TECHNOLOGY AND NATIONALISM

Technology and Nationalism

MARCO ADRIA

McGill-Queen's University Press

MONTREAL & KINGSTON • LONDON • ITHACA

ISBN 978-0-7735-3669-2 (cloth)
ISBN 978-0-7735-3670-8 (paper)

Legal deposit first quarter 2010
Bibliothèque nationale du Québec

Printed in Canada on acid-free paper that is 100% ancient forest free
(100% post-consumer recycled), processed chlorine free

This book has been published with the help of a grant from the Canadian Federation for the Humanities and Social Sciences, through the Aid to Scholarly Publications Programme, using funds provided by the Social Sciences and Humanities Research Council of Canada.

McGill-Queen's University Press acknowledges the support of the Canada Council for the Arts for our publishing program. We also acknowledge the financial support of the Government of Canada through the Book Publishing Industry Development Program (BPIDP) for our publishing activities.

Library and Archives Canada Cataloguing in Publication

Adria, Marco, 1959–
    Technology and nationalism / Marco Adria.

Includes bibliographical references and index.

ISBN 978-0-7735-3669-2 (bnd)
ISBN 978-0-7735-3760-8 (pbk)

    1. Nationalism and technology – Canada.   2. Nationalism – Canada.
3. Regionalism – Canada.   4. Technology – Social aspects – Canada.
5. Internet – Social aspects – Canada.   I. Title.

T14.5.A35 2010   303.48'30971   C2009-905399-3

This book was designed and typeset by Pamela Woodland in Minion 11/14

CONTENTS

ACKNOWLEDGMENTS

I am grateful to colleagues at the University of Alberta for encouraging and supporting my work and to Ghassan Zabaneh for his exploration and discussion with me of optical telegraphy. Portions of the following chapters appeared in different form elsewhere: chapter 2 – *Nations and nationalism: A global historical overview*, vol. 4 (ABL-CIO, 2008); *Canadian Journal of Communication*, vol. 28, no. 2 (2003); and chapter 5 – *British Journal of Canadian Studies*, vol. 21, no. 2 (2008). I wish to thank the publishers for permission to include this material in the book.

TECHNOLOGY AND NATIONALISM

INTRODUCTION

If the Internet represents a new form of univers-
alism, one must understand this not as a closure
of human history, a final realization or telos or
dialectic moving from parochialism to cosmopolitanism. Instead, the Internet globalization suggests an articulation of the universal and particular
at a level at once more general and more local than
the nation-state. In that configuration rest the
prospects for a humanity different from that of
earlier times.

Poster, 1999, 239

Nations cannot be defined effectively by empirical
measures of whether they are actually able to
achieve sovereignty, to maintain integrity by de-
fending themselves against internal splits, or to
enforce sharp boundaries, by whether their culture
is perfectly unified or particularly ancient. Rather,
nations are constituted largely by the claims themselves, by the way of talking and thinking and act-
ing that relies on these sorts of claims to produce
collective identity, to mobilize people for collective
projects, and to evaluate peoples and practices.

Calhoun 1997, 5

Technology and Identity in a World of Nations

Nationalism is part of daily life in Canada as elsewhere. We continually receive the message that we live in a world of nations. National identity is prominently displayed and articulated on special occasions and in extraordinary situations but also as part of our everyday activities and in unremarkable and almost unnoticed ways. British sociologist Michael Billig (1995) argues, in fact, that the most significant displays of national identity are the ones that by their constant appearance become mundane, repetitious, and ubiquitous. National symbols appear at professional sports events, in the newspaper, and even in the broadcasts of the current weather forecast. National flags are reproduced in endless number. We see them draped and displayed prominently on buildings of all kinds, both inside and out, on rooftops, and along the street. Their presence is implied through the colours and symbols of streetscapes, by the appearance and design of shopping centres, and by the organization of the activities making up the typical day at school and work and in the marketplace.

Messages about nationalism arrive through not only the routine use of visible national symbols but also the patterned practices of language. The most profound of the messages of national identity is that we all live in a world of nations. In Canada, the hockey game provides a widely recognizable example. Watching the game, the attention of spectators is drawn to the contest between the "home" and "visiting" teams. This distinction is underlined by the local and national newspaper and television reports of what happened at the game. Included in these reports are references to the sentiments of the "home" audience, in relation to such things as "home-ice advantage." In sport, as in other aspects of everyday life, there is always the distance between "them" and "us" to be taken into account. And "our" national character becomes more intense as the season progresses. Consider the question of whether there may yet be an "all-Canadian" Stanley Cup playoff and the degree to which this question becomes of increasing interest to commentators and fans as the season progresses. The hometown's celebrations inevitably involve not only the symbols of the winning team but that of the winning nation, in particular the Canadian flag. These symbols and practices emphasize and repeat the message, endlessly, that we inhabit and participate in a social world of competition on the one hand and the opportunity for national belongingness on the other.

If the symbols of national identity surround us everywhere, they are to be found in local and regional places and spaces. Here, the national identity must develop some sort of relationship with other identities. It is in this sense that the organizing "logic" of a national identity overlaps with those of regional identities. In some cases, regional and national identities contrast with one another and give rise to conflict; in others, they complement and mutually support one another. Their logic, however, might be expected to be of the same order. The nationalist logic of organizing involves cultural accommodation and homogenization for the purpose of political unity. The means by which the nationalist logic of organizing occurs involves the creation of a single language idiom, accomplished through the adoption and use of communications media and through a standardized system of education. It also involves an emphasis on economic growth through innovation and on the capacity of individuals to move into occupations that require them. At least this is the modernist perspective on the origins of nationalism, one that will be considered in some depth in the following pages.

Within this world of nations appears the internet, a technology used each day by billions of people. New forms of interaction have emerged with the advent of this technology. The basic distinction between face-to-face communication and technology-mediated communication is no longer adequate for capturing the complexity of social action that online technology introduces. These new forms, which are constituted through the "action at a distance" characteristic of mass media, intensify and complicate the formation of national social identities. One of the ways – and an important one, I will argue – that this is occurring in Canada is through the continuing development of regional cultures and the bringing together of the local and the global, in a conflation that Robertson (1995) calls the "glocal." Glocalism is the character of the citizen's existence at once as a subject of the nation-state and as a subject of global media systems. The place of technology in the constitution of the modern citizen is therefore central to nationalism as a structuring influence in the political economy.

Although the internet is relatively new, technology is not. James Carey claims that if, and I would add *only if*, "we adequately place the various technologies of communication in a historical context – not just the history and ecology of technology but the wider world of politics, economics and culture – we may be able to state meaningful and useful (although contingent) generalizations" (Carey 2005, 452). Earlier technologies in history have had an antecedent role in contributing to regional and national social identities, and the internet has intensified and made more visible the identity of the citizen in relation to technology.

A Nationalist Logic of Organizing

"The most important and persistent message is generated by the medium itself, by the role which such media have acquired in modern life," writes Ernest Gellner in *Nations and nationalism*. Here, Gellner reveals an important connection between his influential theory of nationalism, in which the nationalist project is assessed as a consequence of modernity, and the Canadian intellectual tradition concerned with communications and technology. This tradition grew up around the work of Harold Adams Innis, who showed that the fundamental consequence of a technology's widespread use is to be found in reorderings of conceptions of time and space, which are marked by shifts in the organization and relative centralization of administrative power. In this book I want to refine Gellner's theory of nationalism in the context of the Canadian political economy, a context in which regions play a conspicuous role. I will argue that technology and regionalism have together shaped social identity and the nationalist project in Canada. From this perspective, technology is decisively and fatefully entwined with the discursive accomplishment of regional and national identities. Nationalism is the union of cultural nation and administrative state, and technology has been the subject of the English-speaking Canadian cultural idiom by which a progressive, industrialized society has developed.

To explore some of the differences that a technology introduces to what I call a "nationalist logic of organizing" in regional and national spaces, this book presents three Canadian cases, each of which is informed by critical observations of what individuals and groups have said and done within particular historical moments. All three describe the relationship of technology to the nationalist logic of organizing and illustrate the overlapping and mutually influential nature of this logic as it may be observed in regional and national spaces in Canada. The subjects of the cases represent a diversity of technologies, including advanced weapons for national defence, radio broadcasting, and the sociotechnology of new organizations. The cases suggest that (a) the ideological pairing of technology and nationalism has moved the nationalist project along the path of modernity, with technology leading social development in some historical periods and nationalism in others; (b) radio broadcasting in particular established an ontological tension between modernism and antimodernism and in so doing reflected the same conflicting character of nationalism; and (c) the adoption of industrial technology and creation of new organizations has implied an active state that seeks the cultural accommodation required for nationalism as it develops in regional and national spaces. These themes may be viewed as the means by which the book revisits, refines, and to some extent "corrects" Gellner's theory of nationalism, at least in the Canadian case.

Regions are connected to the development of nationalism in Canada by the daily activities of individuals that can be drawn upon as cultural resources in support of the nationalist project. Choices of method and research design always entail tradeoffs, and I chose to aim at validity among the cases. As a consequence, two are from the history of Alberta. This province has been of particular interest to widely influential scholars of Canadian culture and identity. Innis writes about the province in his explorations of regionalism and the relationship of "core" (metropolitan) to "periphery" (hinterland) spaces in Canada (1995). C.B. Macpherson's (1953) examination of the origins of "possessive individualism" begins with his extended study of the political economy of Alberta in the first three decades of the twentieth century. Alberta's culture has formed part of what political scientist David Laycock (1990) calls a tradition of populist democracy. In terms of English-Canada its voice is perennially distinctive on the national scene and has figured, in the work of Roger Gibbins (1992) for example, as a kind of prototypical region. Social identity in the regional space of Alberta has been well developed, and regional alienation has historically been the subject of this identity.

Technology, Region, and the Canadian "Nationalizing State"

This book is about the relationship of local and regional culture, mediated by technology, to a national culture and the development of a national identity. It is a contextualist approach in which a nationalist logic of social organizing is observed to have taken place in regions. Considering historical cases in which technology has been used in the development of social identity can reveal the practices of nationalist organizing and the ways that such a logic combines with commercial, corporate, and bureaucratic logics. Before we proceed to the main argument, three preliminary points should be made. First, technology is defined broadly. Communications media and other technologies are considered together here by the use of the term *technology*. An elision of media into the broader category of technology follows the practice of medium theorists such as Innis (1951), Marshall McLuhan (1964), and, more recently, Ronald Deibert (1997). Ernest Gellner (1983) draws from Innis the fateful insight that media create an environment in which the linguistic idiom of that environment is a required condition of participation in it. The nation coalesces around the shared communication idiom that a technology requires. In McLuhan's interpretation, the Innisian concept of a *medium* is broad indeed. A medium is any "extension of man"; it is the means by which human senses are augmented or amplified. Technology has totalizing effects, and these effects are not limited to communications media. The cases considered in this book present technology as the social stakes for which regions and nations compete. In one of the cases, it is the fate of radio as a technology in Canada. In the case involving Prime Minister Diefenbaker's government, the technology of antiballistic missiles is in play.

Second, as Deibert (1997) points out, the bias or favouring aspects of a technology do not appear spontaneously as individuals abruptly drop certain social preferences and adopt others. Instead, the "web of social preferences" changes over time; they are intergenerational changes, not intrapsychic. Over time, too, technologies that are used intensively may "reverse" their effects, in one historical era helping to create a shared sense of identity and a shared purpose, but in another era encouraging atomism and anomie (see McLuhan and McLuhan 1988).

The role of technology in furthering nationalist projects is an intervening variable in nationalist projects, because of the modern character of nationalism. I will therefore argue in this book that technology is decisively and fatefully entwined with social identity. The culture of the modern nation-state is of a particular kind. It is homogenous, and it is mediated by technology. In this sense, we can refer to "media effects" and to the creation of a mass audience. The newspaper of the eighteenth and nineteenth centuries, for example, created a space for the discussion of ideas and a common language for its transmission, one reflecting the concerns of a high literate culture. But the creation of a high literate culture is not a benign process. Nationalism relies on abstractions of a national past. Information and communications technologies allow for the creation of new texts in which these abstractions are developed, recorded, disseminated, and adapted. These technologies are central to the efforts of social movements and their leaders to establish and maintain the modern nation-state. The consequences of the adoption and use of certain technologies must be examined if we are to understand the social meaning and uses of nationalism. I will describe Canadian nationalism in terms of the union of cultural nation and administrative state and its striving for a common cultural idiom by which a technologically progressive, industrialized society could be developed.

Regional backcurrents of economic, cultural, and political activities exist within regions, provinces, states within federations, and other regional settings within the national configuration of technology and social identity. I will therefore argue not only that technology is fully entwined with social identity but also that technology and regionalism have together shaped social identity and the nationalist project in Canada. The claim is that national identity is a discursive accomplishment between region and nation. Nationalist projects involve not only the initial determination to found a nation-state but also the ongoing process of ensuring that the coupling remains tight between national culture and administrative state. Such projects draw upon the cultural development of regional groups, such as provinces, regions, and states within federations. The likelihood of the eventual success of any one project, and the timing that characterizes its rise (or failure to rise), may be assessed in part in a local or regional context. The national development of social identity draws on the development of social identity in these regional contexts. The social identity of the nation develops in part as regional groups take up *national* cultural issues.

In chapter 1, an overview of the scholarship of nationalism is provided. Contrasting theoretical approaches to nationalism are discussed, with an emphasis on the relationship of Gellner's modernist theory of nationalism to other approaches. The social question addressed in this book is complementary to the political question raised by Gellner, who queried the basis for the nation-state's political legitimacy. The modernist theory of nationalism he developed in response has had a significant influence on sociological and historical accounts of nationalism. It is often the touchstone for further inquiries into the meaning of nationalism. In his writings over a period of three decades, Gellner maintained that nationalism becomes politically acceptable to a large population when it constitutes a route to modernization. The industrialization of societies in history has required a consistent and relatively homogenous culture as its foundation. Such a culture constituted the most acceptable foundation for political legitimacy. The nation as we have come to know it – literate, socially egalitarian, and technologically modern – has provided the political basis for nationalism, one with which we are not, in historical terms, quite finished.

Brian Osborne (2006a) insightfully calls our attention to the open-endedness of the nation-state's involvement in identity construction by writing about the *nationalizing state*, in which never-ending bureaucratic and official activities are carried out to support a preferred national identity. In chapter 2, a historical view is provided of the relationship of technology to the English-speaking national culture in Canada as that of a nationalizing state. The chapter considers the case of "technological nationalism" in Canada, which is the rhetorical use of technology in the development of a national consciousness. The case describes the Canadian Missile Crisis of 1962 and the dialectic between technology and nationalism that may be discerned in the events of that year. Modernism emphasizes the role of communications using technology, mass education, democratic and political participation, and urbanization in the development of society. Modern states have developed as a product of technologically mediated communication. Such technologies were invented in the modern era and their subsequent use has constituted the social character, aesthetic qualities, and administrative methods of modernism.

Since it was fully articulated in 1983 in *Nations and nationalism*, Gellner's approach to nationalism has been critiqued and corrected. Although Gellner persuasively shows that the "why" of nationalism could be linked to modernization, the means of its appearance and growth – the many "how" questions – remain. What are the potential pathways for the nationalizing state? Why does nationalism flourish in some cultural contexts and not in others? And why does it require one nation-state only a few years to come to fruition, while in another national setting it never fully takes hold? These questions take on particular importance when one realizes that nationalisms compete. The modernist explanation for nationalism is that industrialization requires a homogenous culture, but this does not account for the relatively small number of nation-states that have come into being. There are many more nations potentially seeking states than the number of countries in the world. Not every language in the world is associated with a national culture, and not every national culture has aligned itself with a state. The conditions for the rise of nationalism vary significantly. In chapter 3, then, the case is made for giving attention to regional cultural development in the context of technology adoption and use. The conditions for the nationalist logic of organizing in particular regions may be examined to reveal how and in what circumstances the nationalist idea is likely to take root and in what circumstances it is likely to lead to the political union of nation and state and to its ongoing maintenance.

The next two chapters discuss cases of technological development and the relationship of this development to regional and national identity. In these cases, a contextualist concern with the nationalist logic of organizing within a social space – in both instances, a regional Canadian space – is extended. Wiley (2004) suggests that the nationalist logic of organizing may be at work where it may not be expected and that a key task of the analyst is to explain where and how such a logic is active: "[I]nstead of beginning with the nation as place and arguing about what kind of place it is, about the proper way to conceptualize it and engage with it, one could begin with a social space and ask how, or if, or to what extent, it is organized as national." (91) In Canada, regional space is organized as national through a rhetoric of technological progress. In chapter 4, the case of radio broadcasting is examined in the context of its simultaneously modern and antimodern influence on social identity. The case of radio broadcasting in the 1920s and 1930s, and the implications for both regional and national identity it offers, is considered. The voice of the radio's "writer-speaker," as McLuhan characterizes it, carries the capacity both to contribute to the modernization of a society and to uncover and revive its premodern past. Radio's modern form relies on such systems as an electrical grid and on manufacturing methods for the production of receiving devices. It relies as well on modern techniques of social organizing, including the politically fraught process of allocating the radio spectrum. But the writer-speaker, along with the music introduced, evokes the premodern character of social identity through the reliance on oral, rather than textual, methods of communication. The link from the regional to the national level of identity is traced in the chapter through an examination of national broadcasting policy in Canada.

In chapter 5, innovation and occupational mobility, both of which are given prime importance in Gellner's account of nationalism, are discussed in turn. Both are stronger as social forces the closer they are to the urgent and proximate concerns of the population. The regional and the local are therefore potent spaces in which innovation and occupational mobility may be made visible to the population. As Castells (2001) argues, nation-states today are decentralizing as never before, leading to new points of political conflict:

> On the one hand, because of the territorial differentiation of state institutions, regional and national minority identities find their easiest expression at local and regional levels. On the other hand, national governments tend to focus on managing the strategic challenges posed by the globalization of wealth, communication, and power, hence letting lower levels of governance take responsibility

for linking up with society by managing everyday's life issues, so to rebuild legitimacy through decentralization. However, once this decentralization of power occurs, local and regional governments may seize the initiative on behalf of their populations, and may engage in developmental strategies *vis a vis* the global system, eventually coming into competition with their own parent states. (272)

Yet such decentralization has been a fact in Canada for many decades, and ideas for further decentralization continue to bubble up, as in Broadbent's (2008) call for an "urban nation." The case presented in chapter 5, describing a remarkably autonomous and powerful state-sponsored organization, provides evidence of the historical meaning and legacy of Canada's distinctive development of social identity through the deployment of technology. The local and regional "demonstration effect" of the modernist theory of nationalism is a technological event. The establishment of new organizations in a society can provide a tangible example for individuals and groups of the benefits of the nationalist project. Like the other cases, the one presented in this chapter outlines the nationalist logic of organizing that occurs in overlapping regional and national spaces and points to the importance of technology in mediating this overlap.

The role of technology in the development of social identity has barely begun – having been inaugurated with the printing press some five and a half centuries ago. Chapter 6 discusses the most contemporary and pervasive of communications technologies, the internet, and its relationship to the development of regional and national identities. In a somewhat speculative mode, I consider the future of regional technological development and its contributions to the nationalizing state in Canada.

1

EXPLAINING NATIONALISM

> Nationalism ... came as an intense new visual image of group destiny and status, and depended on a speed of information movement unknown before printing.
>
> McLuhan 1964, 161

A nation is a group of people sharing a culture and recognizing one another as fellow nationals. Yet it is impossible to name the defining and originating example of modern national*ism*. As Calhoun writes, "there was no first nationalist." Nationalism appears out of experiments, trials, and false starts, and in revisitations of thought, opinion, argument, polemic, and debate. It is an outcome of rhetorical methods and discursive formations. The story of nationalism emerges in European history out of a constellation of other narratives that, although having some affinities with what would eventually be recognized as modern nationalism, appears at first as only suggestion or foreshadowing. Choosing the words that first embodied the nationalist voice must be accomplished as a disciplined estimate.

The events that may be regarded as providing evidence of the emergence of nationalism as a distinctive discursive formation occurred over a period of centuries. Scholars have settled, variously, on several periods as representing the beginning of nationalism. These include the mid-seventeenth century (the English Civil War and, in 1648, the Peace of Westphalia, which instituted for the first time a European order based on national sovereignty); the final decades of the eighteenth century (the French Revolution); the beginning of the nineteenth century (German unification and the struggles for Latin American independence); and the mid-nineteenth century (the Peace of Versailles in 1919 ending the First World War, based on the principle of national self-determination, and also the Italian *Risorgimento*). The first nationalist project was any or all of these, because modern nationalism began in a parallel relationship with the rise of the form of government that would become known as the nation-state. Over the last several centuries in Europe, the nation-state created itself through territorial claims and then defended itself by warfare (Kedourie 1962). The legislative institutions intended to broker the interests of competing regional powers were an important component of the state power that developed during this period. Parliaments became a key institution of what would become the modern state because they brought with them the capacity to resolve the always-simmering conflicts of intradomain principalities and powers (Lessnoff 2002). Another component of state power coming to prominence was bureaucracy (Weber 1958). Bureaucratic structures arose in support of the monarchy, increasing the territorial reach of the king or queen. Decisions could be carried out more effectively than they could through direct decrees and appointments. Expertise and information could be built up and protected within the state. Monarchies depended on trade for their wealth, and on the political support of the merchant classes that produced this wealth. National identities were developed in order to maintain the legitimacy of this trade (Bruner 2002). By providing a legitimate national home for wealth accumulation, the efforts of the bourgeoisie were enlisted in common economic cause.

The dramatic expansion of the principle of nationalism as an expression of the nation-state's legitimacy occurred in the nineteenth and twentieth centuries, following from the convulsions of the French Revolution (Best 1988), beginning in 1848 and followed by a series of uprisings in other countries sometimes called the "Springtime of the peoples." Germany and Italy were the most prominent of those nascent nations following the path of creating a powerful nation-state. Both were made up of a large number of smaller states, and both were politically unified in the nineteenth century. Political alignment was only the first stage of unification, with cultural accommodation following. The loyalties to the mini-states in Germany and Italy had to be transformed into loyalty to the nation. The state of Florence, for example, had historically enjoyed the allegiance of its inhabitants and of prominent theorists of the state's powers, such as Machiavelli. However, Florence in all of its political glory was not a nation, as Calhoun notes: "It was not until the nineteenth-century 'Risorgimento' that the 'nationalist' idea of unifying all Italians under a single state gained widespread currency" (Calhoun 1997, 7). The task that remained after unification was to "make Italians," because the "Italian citizen" was a new category. Political unification had to be followed by cultural unification. Of course, the process of cultural construction of the national citizen is at odds with the idea of an immemorial and essential national character. The concept of constructing the national identity has been of scholarly interest since B. Anderson's (1996) coining of the now-famous phrase *imagined community*. The construction of the national citizen was prepared by writers and philosophers of the seventeenth century, who called for the drawing out and elevation of the national character. The earliest nationalist histories premised their arguments on the natural right and responsibility of individuals to create a better society by living within a common culture.

The preceding outline of the development of nationalism and the nation-state leaves unanswered some notable questions about how to describe and understand nationalism. We may ask, for example, why nationalism, as distinct from the phenomena of the nation-states described, has flourished as it has over the last three centuries. What were the social and political antecedents for nationalism? And what is the relationship of culture to politics in this history? In terms of causation, should we consider the independent variable to be nations or nationalism? Have nations bided their time over the centuries previous, waiting for the particular political form of nationalism to appear, after which their national aspirations could finally find expression and fulfillment? Or does the structure of the nation-state reach out with its promise of material power to find and keep those national communities that may be recruited to the program of modernity? In short, do nations cause nationalism or does nationalism cause nations?

Most historical and sociological accounts of nationalist movements seek to explain or critique the establishment and maintenance of the modern state in conjunction with a national community. The modernist approach is that nationalism is a political and social configuration, an innovation or invention (O'Leary 1998; Bhabha 1990). Nationalism is the alignment of nation and state, forged in the pursuit of modernization. Not all nations seek their own state, but when conflict erupts out of a sense by members of a minority group that they are on the losing end of the economic stick, a contest over the control of the state can take up the energies of the nationalist movement (Mann 2005).

The modernist lens on nationalism may not be strong enough. It may prevent us from seeing important aspects of nationalism's workings. Refocusing the lens can be accomplished by exploring historical cases in which the practices of nationalist organizing have occurred in local and regional contexts, and the ways that such a nationalist logic combines with other logics, such as those of commerce, corporations, and bureaucracies. The cases suggest a conception of nationalism that differs in a critical respect from the modernist one. They illustrate a logic of political organizing seeking a kind of symbiosis of nation and state, not only in national spaces but also in local and regional spaces. And they lead us to consider technology's historical function in the development of nationalist ideas.

The existence of tensions between region and nation is an important finding of the cases. In chapter 4, for example, such tensions become clear in policy deliberations carried out by the federal government. Some tensions in the cases are implied. There is a direct link between the regional experimentation in healthcare in Canada in the 1950s and the eventual adoption of a national healthcare system in the early 1960s. Tensions have effects, and the effects in this instance have to do with a kind of brokering process that occurs at the national level.

The modernist account to be revisited and in part corrected in this book is based on a materialist worldview. The material basis for the development of nationalism during the last three centuries must be understood in the context of the cultural unity that constitutes the political legitimacy of the nation-state. A nationalist project takes on the potency of a social movement only when it its actions become linked in the minds of many people with a national culture. Technology's relationship to nationalism is both modern and antimodern.

Technology's mediating role allows for the transmission of messages hallowing the ancient glory of the nation. Its demonstrational uses involve highlighting a state's political, economic, and military power in relation to other nations.

Hall (1998) lists three possible trajectories for national identities in the contemporary world: erosion because of cultural homogenization; strengthening through local resistance; and supplantation by new, hybrid identities (300). This chapter describes contrasting theoretical approaches to nationalism with the aim of developing the second of these, the strengthening hypothesis, but in a particular mode – that of the narrative of technological progress within regional spaces. The chapter emphasizes the relationship of Gellner's modernist theory of nationalism to other approaches. It establishes the conceptual basis for a consideration in the subsequent chapter of the particular context for the historical and social nexus of technology and nationalism in Canada. A discussion of the modernist approach will therefore be preceded by a description of the primordial approach to the study of nationalism, which identifies blood ties at the core of the national culture. In this view, culture is a set of ethnic relationships constituting the nation. Modernist nationalist theory will also be compared with perennialism, which is a variation on both the modernist and primordialist approaches. Perennialism conflates ethnicity and nationality, describing national culture as organic and taking different forms in history, with the nation-state only the most recent of these forms. Taken together, primordialism and perennialism differ from modernist accounts in describing nationalist sentiment as existing before the nation-state. They may be contrasted with one another to the extent to that primordialism posits an ideal, immutable core of cultural difference. The chapter will conclude with a consideration of cultural approaches to national identity and a proposal to regard technology in its regional context as a key to understanding nationalism in Canada.

Primordialist and Perennialist Explanations for Nationalism

Prominent among the philosophers of the primordial philosophy of national character were the German Romantic philosophers of the eighteenth century, primarily Johann Gottlieb Fichte (1762–1814) and

Johann Gottfried Herder (1744–1803). For the Romantics, the nation was not "voluntary" but "organic." In the primordial view a natural division of nations exists, and each nation bears self-evident, distinguishing cultural characteristics. Although the nation is not based on voluntary membership, there is a constitutive role in the nation for the individual citizen, which is to affirm citizenship through such simple acts as expressing allegiance to the homeland. The nation is constituted by the citizen through the common activities of work and interaction. The stakes at play in the activities of remembering, commemorating, and constituting the nation are nothing less than the independence and autonomy of the nation. Remembering is thus the primary duty of the nationalist. From time to time, the national culture is weakened as a consequence of its members forgetting their duty to the nation. Nationalist projects are therefore worthy, laudable, and necessary, because they restore the memory and development of the high esteem in which the nation should be held, not only within the national space but as a principle of human community, everywhere in all nations. Fichte argued that in addition to a responsibility to the homeland, the citizen had a moral responsibility to contribute to the corporate efforts of all humanity. Such a contribution must be properly made within the traditions and conventions of the national culture. It was in this spirit that he wrote the *Addresses to the German people* of 1807, which encouraged Germans to revive the fortunes of their country, which had declined since the French Revolution and subsequent invasions by Napoleon. Civilization for Fichte was built on a national framework whose well-developed culture formed the basis for common action: "It is the vocation of our race to unite itself into one single body, all the parts of which shall be thoroughly known to each other, and all possessed of similar culture. Nature, and even the passions and vices of men, have from the beginning tended towards this end; a great part of the way towards it is already passed, and we may surely calculate that this end, which is the condition of all further social progress, will in time be attained!" (1931, 120).

In world affairs, the principle and practice of developing the autonomous nation, organized within the administrative facility of the state, would lead to international harmony, because the legitimate and civilized nation had no interest in meddling in the affairs of another nation: "Soon will the nations, civilized or enfranchised by them, find themselves placed in the same relation towards others still enthralled by barbarism or slavery, in which the earlier free nations previously stood towards them, and be compelled to do the same things for these which were previously done for themselves; and thus, of necessity, by reason of the existence of some few really free states, will the empire of civilization, freedom, and with it universal peace, gradually embrace the whole world" (ibid., 125).

Through the primordialist lens, the state had the role of finding psychic space for the expression of what already existed, which was the ancient and divine spirit of the people. In Kedourie's words, the primordial view is that "the state should be the creator of man's freedom not in an external and material sense, but in an internal and spiritual sense" (1962, 47).

Herder has been considered the founder of cultural nationalism, because he felt that each culture should exult in its difference. He conceived of political identity as being rooted in a national culture, or *volk*. His was a particularist philosophy in which national difference was to be celebrated. At the same time, Herder was a universalist, calling for an affirmation of all forms of national life and expression. His harshest criticism was reserved for compatriots who castigated German culture while adopting French customs and affectations. He argued that sharing a common culture allowed for political coordination and administration to be accepted as legitimate by a population. For Herder, the source of a national culture was language. The *volk*-state becomes possible when people holding, recognizing, and sharing a common culture adopt an administrative and legal regime to govern themselves. The state itself must remain as an impersonal shell for that purpose. It is the nation's common culture, not the state itself, that gives life to the nation-state. National difference for Herder arises in part from the geographical factors shaping the culture and also from the cultural institutions and practices of education and tradition. However, the defining characteristic of a national culture is its language, and Herder's main contribution to theories of nationalism was the centrality of language. An individual becomes aware of both selfhood and nationhood through language. Language provides the source of the variety of cultural life. Conflict is an indispensable part of the process by which that variety achieves continuity in time: "The Egyptian detests the shepherd and the nomad and despises the frivolous Greek. Similarly prejudices, mob judgment and narrow nationalism arise when the dispositions and spheres of happiness of two nations collide. But prejudice is good, in its time and place, for happiness may spring from it. It urges nations to converge upon their centre, attaches them more firmly to their roots, causes them to flourish after their kind, and makes them more ardent and therefore happier in their inclinations and purposes" (Herder 1969, 186).

The German Romantics' philosophy was to be extended in the twentieth century in the ideology of nationalist leaders. The primordial view of national culture has become only a secondary concern of nationalist scholars, in part because of the violent consequences of its use by nationalists in Eastern Europe. However, the cultural roots of nationalist movements cannot be ignored, and in Canada the philosopher George Grant was to take up the spirit, if not the texts, of the German Romantics in calling for "loving our own" as a first principle of cultural development (Grant 1965; Emberley 1990).

Through the perennialist approach, most notably the work of Anthony J. Smith (2000), the enduring character of national cultures, as described by Fichte and Herder, is still a subject of inquiry in nationalist studies. Unlike the principle of primordialism, perennialism does not regard blood ties as the basis for the national identity. Instead, it conflates ethnicity and nationality, suggesting that a cultural community is immemorial, an organic entity that has taken different forms in recorded history. Perennialism describes a national culture as having adopted the nation-state as only the most recent of these forms: "Ethnicity has always been experienced as a kinship phenomenon, a continuity within the self and within those who share an intergenerational link to common ancestors" (Fishman 1980, 84). For the perennialist, nationalism is new but nations are not. The narratives given voice in a national culture are of interest to the study of nationalism, because stories about the status of the nation suggest the social trajectory of the nationalist project. Narratives about the national "home" for its citizen are created out of the modern notion of domesticity, with its emphasis on privacy and comfort (Manning 2003). Likewise, the story of victimhood, which recounts the ways in which the nation suffers, often gives life to nationalism at a particular stage of its development

(Bruner 2002). The perennialist suggests therefore that nationalism is a modern and updated administrative form within which an ancient culture takes shape. The state is not the first vessel in which the nation has resided, and there may be another in the future.

The Modernist Explanation for Nationalism and Its Critics

With the publication of *Nations and nationalism* in 1983, Ernest Gellner posed and answered the question of why the political legitimacy of nationalism was established so decisively in many countries, especially in the nineteenth and twentieth centuries. His theory of nationalism was grounded in a materialist interpretation of history. He argued that industrialization requires just the kind of cultural homogeneity that nationalist projects require. Gellner proposed that the goals of industrialization and nationalism had merged in history. The modernist view of the emergence of nationalism is therefore that the requirements of industrial society introduce a measure of cultural homogeneity that is coincident with the unifying call of nationalist sentiment. The fertile and paradigmatic thesis was, in short, that *nationalism causes nations*, and not the reverse.

The theory required a description of industrial society's primary features. Gellner noted that industrial society is characterized by growth and indeed that it *requires* perpetual growth for its continued existence. Agrarian society's social roles were stable and subject only to slow and incremental change. Premodern social processes had been allocational. Individuals were streamed early in life to their respective social stations – some to labour, others to farming and animal husbandry, and still others to servitude. There was no inherent need for all individuals to acquire the capacities of reading and writing. But in the modern period the requirement for universal literacy becomes urgent. "Every man a clerk," writes Gellner about the modern break with social allocation. With mass education, the illiterate come to constitute a very small minority within modern societies.

In industrial society, there is constant technological innovation and a continuous redefinition of social roles. In particular, the occupation of an individual may vary within social classes and within individual lifetimes. Such a society encourages social mobility, because mobility allows for the distribution of individuals where and as they are required to accommodate industrial growth. It is a marked variation on pre-modern social allocation because individuals now voluntarily accept the opportunities opened up by new occupations in society as these are eliminated or reduced in status. Gellner's account of nationalism departs from primordialist explanations in its concern to show that the elements of a culturally unifying nationalism are favourable to the requirements of industrialization and, in turn, to an adaptive and aspiring population: "[I]n a hectically mobile society, custom has no time to hallow anything. A rolling stone gathers no aura, and a mobile population does not allow any aura to attach to its stratification. Strat-ification and inequality do exist, and sometimes in extreme form; nev-ertheless, they have a muted and discrete quality, attenuated by a kind of gradualness of the distinctions of wealth and standing, a lack of social distance and a convergence of lifestyles, a kind of statistical or probabilistic quality of the differences (as opposed to the rigid, abso-lutised, chasm-like differences typical of agrarian society), and by the illusion or reality of social mobility" (1983, 25).

The means by which nationalism takes root in a society is connected in Gellner's theory to the Marxist concept of uneven development. But there is a crucial difference. For Marx, cleavages in economic devel-opment led to divided, not united, nations. Gellner argued that nation-alism appeared and flourished at those stages in the development of a political association in which the benefits of modernization were felt to be unfairly distributed. Nationalism emerged when the political principle of "one state, one culture" was violated: "[N]ationalism is a phenomenon connected not so much with industrialization or mod-ernisation as such, but with its uneven diffusion. The uneven impact of this wave generates a sharp social stratification which, unlike the stratifications of past societies, is a) unhallowed by custom ... b) is not well protected by various social mechanisms ... and which c) is reme-diable, and is seen to be remediable, by 'national' secession" (Gellner 1965, 166). With uneven industrial development, the humiliation of living as a cultural stranger leads to social tensions that in some instances foreshadow the creation of a fully fledged nationalist move-ment. Uneven development has been characteristic of economic activity since ancient times and has led to cataclysmic consequences for minority groups. During the period of European colonization, the sharp imbalances in power and trade between the colonizers and the colonized were part of the precipitating conditions for genocide (Mann 2005). The basic principle of group formation is that it "often occurs in the face of uncertainties of physical security and food production" (Hechter 2001, 20). For Gellner, nationalism's roots are to be found in the profound changes in society that occurred during industrialization of the eighteenth and nineteenth centuries. During this time, manufacturing, mechanization, and international commerce developed from a revolution in social communications and the universalization of standardized education. Technology was at the heart of this revolution, allowing for the rapid exchange of ideas and for the archiving and preservation of texts.

The consequences of nationalism were a determination to pursue economic growth and through this a commitment to vertical and social mobility, as well as to a high literate culture, which acts as the common medium between nation and state. Gellner points out that education in this sense is crucial in the development of national movements for its role in upholding the values of the intelligentsia: "Transitional societies are societies which have ceased to be viable, subjectively and objectively: their norms can no longer be effectively internalised, and their external arrangements can no longer be sustained – either through the direct impact of modern institutions, or through the sheer 'demonstration effect' of a measurelessly richer and more powerful alien world. Education, in such a context, is in effect the accentuation, acceleration, of this perception, and the equipment of its possessor with a means of more clearly conceiving, and working towards, an alternative" (1965, 170).

Education is also important in the creation of elites. The well-educated group in the disadvantaged region, "though discontented, will remain within the larger society, either awaiting the moment when the high tide of prosperity reaches it as well, or anticipating events by large-scale migration" (Gellner 1965, 167). Ideologies are developed as individuals and groups seek broadly encompassing accounts of how their interests may be protected and advanced. A distinguishing mark of nationalism is the imposition of a high culture on society (Gellner

1994). Gramsci describes the same phenomenon when he states that, "the supremacy of a social group manifests itself in two ways, as 'domination' and as 'intellectual and moral leadership'" (1971, 57). The socialization of individuals to a common social identity is central to the tasks of the state, because the modern path to industrialization requires it.

In Gellner's theory of nationalism, then, nations become a consequence of nationalism through these means: *literacy, education, communications media, innovation,* and *occupational mobility.* Gellner's political definition of nationalism is that nationalism is a doctrine calling for each nation to be ruled within its own state. Paradoxically, his theory of nationalism is weak in its political premises. As a result, there has been no shortage of criticism of the theory. Gellner engaged most of these before his death in 1996 (see, for example, Hall and Jarvie 1996). These criticisms generally raise two major questions. First, there is the question of functionalism. The theory can be criticized for its tendency to explain historical events as anticipating, in an unexplained fashion, later historical outcomes (P. Anderson 1996); Laitin 1998a; Mann 1996). The modern nation tautologically evolves out of its tendency to take on the characteristics of what would become the modern nation. What is missing is the intention and conscious work of actors involved – political leaders, writers, intellectuals – in building the nation-state. These actors' intentions are generally concerned with non-economic issues, and in particular the cultural issue of cultivating the view of the nation as a primordial entity. They cannot therefore be considered to be knowledgeable about their contribution to the alignment of nation and state in the pursuit of industrialization. The causality of Gellner's theory has been criticized for relying on a functional logic.

Gellner defended his position on causality by arguing that a functionalist analysis is not necessarily teleological. He noted that one can describe the *mechanisms* that link the functional requirements of industrialization with the emergence and consolidation of a literacy-linked, context-free nationalist idiom. Gellner also confirmed that there were indeed two explanatory aspects to be considered at once in his theory: the cultural requirements common to both nationalism and industrialization, and the work of social actors who brought nationalism to life in a given social context. Both were needed. The politicians and others who brought nationalism to a particular part of the world reflected the contingency of the theory. Nationalism emerged as a consequence of material conditions, but the manner in which this happened depended on the variables of history. Not all cultures or language communities were destined to achieve their own nation-state. Many were not capable of doing so, and still others would not even make the attempt. Of those that did try, only a few would be successful. A nuanced account of the varying conditions under which nationalism actually emerged in history is provided by Lessnoff (2002), who argues that the nation-state first developed in Britain and France, with other nation-states, beginning with Germany and Italy, developing in *response* to the economic power of the older nation-states. The power of Gellner's theory to reveal the broadest significance of nationalism – along with the account it provided for the legitimacy of the nation-state – has been largely undiminished by the critiques regarding causality. Theoretical innovation in nationalist studies continues to take into account Gellner's insight regarding the modern character of nationalism (Taylor 1993, 1998).

The second criticism of Gellner is related to the first, in that it asks about the cultural knowledge and aspirations of individuals who actually work out the implications of nationalist projects. The criticism is that culture is given an inappropriately minor status in Gellner's account. Critics have stated that the modernist theory of nationalism suggests, wrongly, that what happened in the development of nationalism in particular cultural contexts is unimportant (O'Leary 1998; Smith 1998). Yet culture provides the raw material for nationalist movements. Without the fellow-feeling of culture, nationalism becomes only a political and economic project, one that is unlikely even in the best of circumstances to attract the support of large numbers of the population.

Gellner responded that the modernist theory of nationalism was unaffected by the actions of nationalists and their ideas. The work of actors in particular national contexts might be of passing interest and capable of adding local colour to the narrative of particular nationalisms, but it was not essential to the theory. Local actors cannot change the historical circumstances in which they find themselves. These circumstances are constituted most critically by the fact that the nation-state provides the only pathway to modernization. No other route to modernization exists, Gellner claimed, and even those nationalists with a belief in the potency of their own nation must accept the limits of their individual power and even that of their national polity. Nationalists are thus free to choose and pursue nationalism or to ignore it. They do not have the ability to change the force of history. Gellner never acceded to the criticism around culture; nor did he modify his views in response. Critics adopting a cultural perspective on nationalism, as noted in the next section, have provided possible responses to the questions raised.

Culture, Technology, and Nationalist Strategies

Gellner's account of nationalism suggests the hegemonic work that is characteristic of nationalist activities by pointing to the interplay of authentically felt cultural identity and the deployment of that culture for defined political purposes. Cultural theories of identity, too, provide a critical perspective on nationalism. They remind us that we are dealing with deeply rooted issues of individual development, beginning with childhood and the discovery of the "Other" (Lacan 1981). The concept of "identity" helps to explain how individuals become members of social groups, including national groups. The activity of defining "difference" for oneself, and for the group with which affinities are developed, is continuous throughout a lifetime and underlies the creation of nations and nationalisms.

Identity is developed along two dimensions (Hall and Du Gay 1998). The first of these involves discourses. Discursive practices contribute to conceptions of a group's differences in relation to other groups (Calhoun 1997). Discursive practices "speak to us or hail us into place" (Hall 1998, 5); thereafter we see ourselves as actors within narratives or stories that are established by discursive practices. In Althusser's (1984) terms, individuals are "interpellated," or projected, into discourses as they respond unmindfully to the imperative questioning of a discourse. The second of these dimensions is the more active, subjective work that individuals carry out in finding a place within discourses. Individuals retain some autonomy within discursive accounts, and some movement between social classes, for example, is possible. These two dimensions of identity remain conceptually separate because each presupposes the other. Hall refers to the "suturing" that takes place to allow for the coexistence of the two dimensions in the lives of individuals and groups (1998, 4).

The dual nature of identity – involving objective elements of social structure and subjective ones involving relatively autonomous action – is to be observed in all places and at all times. It is a part of the development of "difference" for both individuals and groups. It is also to be seen in the political work of revolutions, as Gramsci notes in his comments about the *Risorgimento*: "A study of how these innovating forces developed, from subaltern groups to hegemonic and dominant groups, must therefore seek out and identify the phases through which they acquired: 1. autonomy *vis-à-vis* the enemies they had to defeat, and 2. support from the group which actively or passively assisted them; for this entire process was historically necessary before they could unite in the form of a state" (1971, 53). The cultural accommodations that Gramsci describes in Italy in the mid-nineteenth century, and which are relevant as well to German nationalism earlier in the century, provide the clearest evidence of the capacity of nationalism to instill the goal of political unity in large populations.

. The modernist approach has provided a rich view of why nationalism has become the widely accepted mode of state legitimacy over a historical period of only a few centuries. However, it does not explain the variations in how that logic has played out in various historical contexts. The intentions of key actors and groups in initiating and building a nationalist project are absent in the modernist approach to nationalism, as is an explanation of why nationalism did not develop in all times and places that it might have done. In the Canadian case, modernist theory does not account for the negotiation of social identities within the political economy of confederalism.

Van den Bossche is among those who have found Gellner's response on intentionality and local cultural strategies to be unsatisfactory. He argues that Gellner's theory was successful on its own terms in reducing the behaviours of individuals and groups to large-scale social processes. The theory was reductionist in analytical purpose, but that did not justify a proscription of further theoretical consideration of how and why nationalism unfolded in local contexts: "[Gellner] aimed to explain social change within the large framework of history, with reference to structure and organisation. The rather hurt tone with which he replied to his critics suggests his puzzlement, in particular with their repetition of the charge of reductionism. In fact, this is precisely what he set out to do: to reduce particular behaviours of any (group of) individual(s), local contents of ideology and a myriad of local circumstances to their structural characteristics so that the external logic of modernity could be exposed" (van den Bossche 2003, 494).

Mouzelis (1998) outlines the steps in Gellner's argument in an attempt to demonstrate that there is in fact a logical gap into which the actions and strategies of local actors should find a place. These steps are (a) the specialized labour and unstable occupational structure, which lead to (b) the high culture and universal literacy required to maintain such a structure, which are followed by (c) the collective decision of a humiliated population to create its own nation, rather than simply giving up and adopting the dominant "literacy-linked" idiom. Mouzelis points out that neither causality nor intentionality – the second of the dimensions of identity discussed by Hall – is revealed in such a sequence. Instead, he argues that in order to provide causal links between the three steps in particular countries, "it is necessary to bring into the analysis not only vague 'meanings' but *real* actors, playing *specific* games" (Mouzelis 1998, 161). The intentions and motivations of nationalist leaders and thinkers may be explained, of course, by their interest in gaining or maintaining power. Those holding power have the motivation to create or maintain the nationalist project in order to protect their own interests. However, this is an explanation so broad that it does not allow for observation and description in any particularity that would render it meaningful. The spectre of manipulative nationalist instigators is too obvious a solution to the problem. Neither does it allow for the development of predictive generalizations. Van den Bossche argues that the "will to power" is too all-encompassing as an explanation in part because it does not help us to understand why local actors chose one strategy over another. In addition, the attribution to these actors of the knowledge that the nationalist "card" was the best in the circumstances assumes knowledge and expertise that it is not likely they actually held. Furthermore, "the truism [of power-hungry nationalists] cannot but fail to take into account those very contexts in which the strategies have been selected out of a range of possible options, formulated and then implemented ... [T]hose contexts cannot begin to yield an explanation unless they are both historically and socially defined" (van den Bossche 2003, 496).

The cultural strategies employed by nationalists in their national and regional contexts are being taken up in the work of van den Bossche and others. Smith (2000) argues, in what he calls an ethnosymbolic approach, that cultural factors are too strong to be ignored, that culture must be at the centre of any nationalist project, and that the features of cultures differ to an extent that resists the generalization inherent in the modernist theory of nationalism. Nationalism in this sense is far from being an abstract, benign social field. The symbols constituting the national culture have quite pragmatic uses in politics. For Smith, the "ability to call on a rich and well documented 'ethno-history' was to prove a major cultural resource for nationalists, and myths of origins, ethnic election and sacred territories, as well as memories of heroes and golden ages, were crucial to the formulation of a many-stranded ethno-history. All this points to the importance of social memory" (1998, 192).

With memory we return to the German Romantics. Without the passion engendered by a shared culture, nationalism is hollowed out. Its proponents may plead for administrative and economic autonomy but not for a human home for the nation. National affinities are a necessary antecedent for nationalism. The cultural cohesion of the nation results in a search for the administrative power of the state, which takes the form of a kind of shell within which national autonomy may be enacted. In its encounter with modernity, a nation's memories, myths, values, and traditions are rediscovered, exchanged, and developed (Appiah 1996; Mackey 1999). Smith's use of the term *ethnies* (ethnic communities) refers to the perennial and continuous existence of a body of symbols corresponding to a self-recognizing group. It is not the primordial myth of ancestral descent, blood ties, and kinship that provides the common heritage of the nation, but the myth of a shared, historically continuous culture.

Some symbols are more important than others in the development of a national identity. Foremost among the symbols of a national culture is the myth of beginning, which Smith has called a *mythomoteur*, or constitutive political myth (1987, 58). The *mythomoteur* refers to some specified origin in place and time that is thought by nationalists to be unique to the culture. The nation's mythical origin is "essential for the sense of ethnic community, since it marks the foundation point of the groups history, and hence its individuality" (Smith 1981, 66). The life-cycle of the nation is another important myth. Ong (1967) notes that nations are conceived of as human lives, with a "rise and fall," often associated with "health" at some stages and "malaise" or "illness" at others. Ong suggests that social attitudes and structures follow our use of the metaphor of the life-cycle in relation to the nation. For example, the doctrine of apartheid was supported, Ong argues, by a view of race that is cyclical and closed. The integrity of one race in this view may be fatally tainted by intermingling with another. Ong suggests that the adoption of a different metaphor would be followed by different social relations: "We need to replace the cyclic model with some sort of open model more responsive to historical fact. To conceive of the realities of national existence we need perhaps something like the models used by geneticists in thinking of biological populations or by taxonomists in describing the patterns of organic evolution" (1967, 91). The life-cycle myth in Canada has often been given expression in *arboreal* figures, those of forest, roots, the maple leaf, and lonely pines (Osborne 2006a), an alternative for which Manning (2003) has suggested the *rhizomatic*, which depicts something of the multiplicity and mutability of the national culture.

To the myth of beginning and of the life-cycle must be added, albeit less prosaically, the myth and uses of technology. Technology influences, and is influenced by, social strategies of cultural development, conflict, and accommodation. Political and economic elites draw on cultural resources as they are made available for this purpose. These resources become the antecedents of nationalism, and they include, as Gellner established, literacy, education, communications media, innovation, and occupational mobility. Communications technologies are at the centre of the deployment of cultural resources in the pursuit of nationalist projects. They are required for the establishment and maintenance of the modern nation-state.

We may also say that technology is a broader category within which modernism limns the nationalist project. We may observe in the development of nationalism and the nation-state, which takes in the regional field of social action, an interplay among the antecedents of nationalism. Technology as symbol and social practice allows for an interchange between elite and population about the status and trajectory of the regional culture in relationship to the culture of the nation.

In this way, technology constitutes discursive practices that, in Hall's phrase, "speak to us or hail us into place" (1996). In the next chapter, the myth of technology is examined for its influence on the development of Canadian social identity. I will show that technology has existed in a mutually influential relationship with nationalism throughout Canada's history and that this relationship continues to inform the development of both Canadian regional and national social identities today.

2
TECHNOLOGY AND NATIONAL
IDENTITY IN CANADA

It is not just that the language risks losing its expressive power if it is not involved in the achievements of technology, the economy, and so on; it is also that the community cannot be without achievements in these sectors, because these are the sectors that today's people value; and a community without realizations of this kind will inescapably come to deprecate itself and thus find its identity undermined.

Taylor 1993, 49–50

Modernism provides a lens through which we may view the political legitimacy of nationalist projects. Technology is symbolically and substantively associated with all aspects of modernity. For example, the application of technology and of technocratic methods in the school system, and beyond to higher education, is part of the modernist project and therefore inextricably bound up with the process by which a society comes to accept nationalism as its preferred route to modernization. Scientific, technological, technocratic, and social innovation are fostered within modern states as a means of establishing the modern character of the nation and also proposing to the population the continuing benefits of rule by co-nationals.

Nationalism's legitimacy is based on the relationship established between a national culture on the one hand and the administrative and governing capacities of the state on the other. From the principle of political legitimacy follows the modernist definition of nationalism, which is the congruence between the political and national units. Such a definition leaves aside the question of which political unit is likely find its own state and under which conditions it might do so. It does not allow us to predict which nations will successfully find congruence with a state. The modernist approach takes the study of nationalism up and away from idiomatic and particularist explanations of nationalisms and their association with a single ethnic identity.

The powerful nation-states of Italy and Germany, which developed in the eighteenth and nineteenth century, recognized the rights of citizens who were not descended from the dominant ethnic group. The national culture of the nation-state is accommodational. It is accomplished as a product of a discourse of ethnic plurality. Technology has a signal role in contributing to the accommodation required for the creation and maintenance of a nation. Communications media, for example, help make nationalism possible through the creation of a national cultural idiom. The first nation-states, and most since then, were not constituted by a single ethnicity. Ethnic identity has certainly been part of the nation-state's basis for its discursive development. Co-nationals have to speak in one language, or at most in two or three, and the construction of the national identity draws on a relatively small number of ethnic histories and traditions. However, the basis for achieving political unity in a national state has been swept along by the requirements of industrialization, and regional and ethnic identities have had to find a place within the modern requirements of nationalism. These requirements begin with the citizen educated in the basic language skills of the nation and in the norm of social mobility. The modern liberal principle of pluralism has made ethnic distinctions for the purpose of nation-building problematic not only in ethical terms but also in practical terms. Technology serves to fill the gap created by the problem of pluralism by operating at the centre of a discourse of modernity, cultural homogeneity, and industrial progress.

In this chapter, technology adoption in support and consolidation of a national culture is considered. Historical examples from the

Netherlands, Indonesia, France, the US, and Hungary are used to illustrate this phenomenon. These examples also serve to reflect the "invention," or retrospective adoption, of national culture. A historical account is then provided of the relationship of technology to the Canadian national culture. "Technological nationalism" (Charland 1986) refers to the rhetorical use of technology in the development of a national consciousness. The case of the Canadian Missile Crisis of 1962, along with the dialectic between technology and nationalism that it reveals, illustrates and elaborates on the concept of technological nationalism. The Canadian context for the relationship of technology to nationalism will inform the next chapter's proposal for a model of a nationalist logic of organizing in regions.

Technology and Nationalism in the Modern Nation-State

Technology supports and extends nationalisms in some contexts but separates national groups in others. The historical differentiation of the Dutch people from the North Germans, for example, was supported by the special importance of dikes and low-lying tracts of land in Holland during the Middle Ages (Deutsch 1966). The dikes kept water out of the agricultural plots but required systems of pumping and maintenance. Family farms and communities were arranged around these systems. The technological innovation of the dike therefore helped maintain a separate way of life for the Dutch, because it required patterns of work and social life that had at their centre the maintenance of distinctive agricultural methods.

Technology may bolster and support the authority of elites in the promotion of nationalism, as aeronautical technology did for the Indonesian nationalist government of the 1970s and 1980s (Amir 2004). The optical telegraph provides an instance in which the efforts of the state were directed toward extending the national meaning of the technology. The optical telegraph had its imaginative beginnings in 1684, when the British philosopher and physicist Robert Hooke wrote of his desire "to communicate one's mind at distances in as short a time" (Headrick 2003, 123). A number of devices that took the form of what would become the telegraph were invented. In 1793, Claude Chappe in France successfully sent a message using an optical telegraph. The device consisted of a system of pulleys and arms on a tower that could be adjusted to correspond to a code representing the letters of the alphabet. Towers of this kind were built along a line of sight over the landscape. With the invention of the optical telegraph, it became possible for the first time to transmit a message without physically transporting it. Although inventors prior to Chappe had been successful in transmitting and receiving messages, these devices failed to take hold because of a lack of favourable political and social conditions. The political and the social atmosphere after the French Revolution in 1789 provided a fertile ground for new inventions. The association of technology with the national character was expressed by Lakanal, a scientist charged with evaluating Chappe's invention: "What brilliant destiny do science and the arts not reserve for a republic which, by the genius of its inhabitants, is called to become the nation to instruct Europe" (quoted in Standage 1999, 12).

The French Government quickly invested large sums of money to develop and use the optical telegraph, which allowed for more efficient military and governmental correspondence. Significantly, Chappe saw the capacity of the optical telegraph for maintaining the social cohesion of the republic's population. The optical telegraph, even before the wide availability of the newspaper, was providing the kind of coordination required for the emergence of modern nationalism. The recognition by the French Government and military of the advantages of the optical telegraph led to rapid adoption and a monopoly over the use of the technology throughout the country. The state's financial and political investment required to establish Chappe's optical telegraphy was significant. Technological change on a broad scale requires the political and social will to make economic and social investments. These investments constitute a realignment of segments of society. As Zabaneh (2005) notes, such inventions "have the potential to disrupt the status quo of a social order, by requiring a major alignment and adjustment of wide segments of society, demanding an equal presence of readiness from society to undertake such adjustment – in the case of the optical telegraph, the French Revolution and the soaring of French nationalism brought by the creation of the republic." By the late 1700s, the use of the optical telegraph had spread throughout Europe to Sweden, Denmark, and Spain. With the invention of the *electrical* telegraph, the speed and capacity of telegraphy gave rise to the capacity for more users and potentially more efficiencies. The growth and development of the telegraph network was coordinated in order to achieve an international network in terms of the prices for service, allocation of revenues, and privacy rights, as well as technological standards. The conflicts and concerns regarding control of the telegraph's infrastructure by nation-states raised the question of whether an open or closed system would prevail in Europe (Winseck and Pike 2007). Yet the French Government was unwilling at first to give up on a domestic technology for what it considered to be a foreign one. In 1847, the Interior minister of France was quite explicit about the telegraph's essentially political uses (Lubrano 1997, 99; Winseck and Pike 2007, 16). The optical telegraph illustrates how technology becomes associated with national cohesiveness in ways that involve changes to economic and social structures. By the 1850s, France had joined other nations in adopting the electrical telegraph, but for several years France continued to use the older technology while other countries had adopted the new one.

In the US, the formation of national unions revealed something of the nationalizing influence of the electric telegraph. Gabler (1988) notes that only three national labour unions were formed in the 1850s; however, as the electric telegraph was established across the US during the 1860s and 1870s, thirty-one national labour unions were formed: "Sectional conflict, the reintegration of a chastised South into the Union, and an increasingly powerful and activist federal government did much to make labour leaders think nationally. So did the shifting economic emphasis from local to national markets. And no industry better represented this crucial change than the telegraph, no firm better than the Western Union" (146).

As each communications technologies in history has come into widespread use, the promise of that technology for a new era of a more direct democracy has been extolled. The ideal of ancient Greece's direct dialogue between ruler and ruled resurfaces as the telegraph, radio, television, and internet emerged as technologies that would find a place in most households. In Canada, for example, William Aberhart and E.A. Corbett were able to demonstrate the possibilities of radio for direct democratic participation, as will be discussed in chapter 4.

Technologies have been interpreted in different ways by different groups in history. We may look to Europe and the early days of radio for an example of a medium having a social meaning quite different from the one that emerged in North America over the decades. Telefon Hirmondó operated in Budapest, Hungary, from 1893 until about 1916. It was a closed-loop telephone system with some 6,200 subscribers. It was sometimes referred to at the time as the "telephone newspaper" or "news teller." Telefon Hirmondó was used for broadcasting concerts, speeches, and other events that were thought to be uplifting and culturally high-minded, but also for information that people might need in their day-to-day lives. A daily program of broadcasts was published and listeners could use their telephone to hear news about the financial markets, the railway schedule, news from Parliament (the Reichsrath), or an address by the sovereign. A contemporary observer described the broadcast program this way:

> A complete programme is tacked to the wall above each subscribers's receiver, and a glance at this tells just what may be expected at any hour, every day except Sundays and holidays having the same programme. The issue begins at 10.30 AM and ends about 10.30 PM unless a concert or some other night event is being reported, when it keeps on till later. Stock exchange hours are: AM – 10 to 10.30, 11 to 11.15, 11.30 to 11.45. These reports reach subscribers several hours ahead of the evening papers. Quotations are given again in the afternoon, while reports of the *Reichsrath* and political news occupy the time from 11.45 to 12. When the *Reichsrath* is not in session, the time is filled by fuller reports of general and foreign news. General news of course comes all day at intervals. At 1.30 and at 6 PM is a brief résumé for those who missed the first news. From 5.00 to 6.00 there are concerts, varied by literary criticism, sporting events, and so on. Special items for Sunday are: 11 to 11.30 – news, 4.30 to 6.00 – a concert, and every Thursday evening at six there is a concert for children. The writer was invited to witness a performance in the concert room of *Hirmondó*, but unfortunately a violent thunder storm interfered with the use of the wires. (Denison 1901, 641)

An English journalist commented at the time that if a system similar to Telefon Hirmondó were to be reproduced in other countries, the "humblest cottage would be in immediate contact with the city, and the 'private wire' would make all classes kin" (Crowley and Heyer 1999, 212). Experiments with the system took place in New York City, but these were eventually overcome by the commercial model of radio broadcasting. Television, too, has had proponents who wanted to use the new medium to educate and enlighten the population. The internet is promoted as a medium in which direct democracy might be enacted.

The influence of technology on the development of nationalism has been of particular interest in the context of European-colonized communities. In the European colonies, technology was at once the means by which the colony was established and the pathway to its dismantling. Rather than using military force and the deployment of a large part of its population to warfare, the European conquest of many parts of the world in the eighteenth and nineteenth centuries relied on the technology of trade and industry. A complex of literacy, a universal postal system, railways, and government subsidies for the postal delivery of newspapers contributed to this conquest (Osborne and Pike 2004). Colonized peoples were conquered through the new economic and cultural technologies of train and telegraph, rather than the older methods of fortress and firepower. The adoption and deployment of technology in colonial countries had consequences that neither the colonized nor the colonizers could anticipate. Colonized countries were lost to their respective empires throughout the twentieth century, but principally between 1905 and 1960. The advances of transportation, communication, and production, which colonizing powers introduced into Latin America, the East Indies, Africa, and other regions, allowed for the effective harnessing of local natural resources and human energies. However, the diffusion of even the most sophisticated of technologies leads to adoption, exploitation, and improvement by local populations in ways that colonizers could not predict. Native populations in colonies were employed to operate the factories, trains, and radio and telegraph transmitters. The authority of colonizing political elites was reduced as it became clear that a monopoly over the use of technology could not be maintained indefinitely. Technology was interpreted and used by colonizers to display their advanced capacity to administer and organize the colonized lands for the purpose of enhanced trade. It was also used to support and protect imperial culture, maintaining the native culture as a museum specimen (Mackey 1999). For colonized peoples, technology was interpreted as a means of improving living standards and reviving native ways of life.

In the late colonial landscape of Dutch Indonesia, leading up to the invasion by Japan in 1942 and the subsequent independence of the country, radio had a conspicuous role in both encouraging an indigenous culture for the native population and in connecting the colonists to home (Mrázek 2002). Differing metaphors for radio broadcasting were adopted by the native Indonesians on the one hand and by the colonial Dutch on the other. For the native community, radio provided a means of developing a regional musical identity, as it did with kroncong, a popular genre of Hawaiian-style song. Kroncong was favoured by not only the native Indonesians but by other surrounding native cultures, including the Chinese. The medium represented casual entertainment, popular cultural development, and diversion for the native Indonesians. For the colonists, by contrast, radio was an unseen telephone cable from the colonized country to the homeland of the Netherlands. It was a means of maintaining Dutch cultural isolation within Indonesia. Radio featured news from the homeland, expressions of musical and literary tradition, and cultural uplift. A historical view of other technologies in the colony, including roads, buildings, optical technologies, and media, allows an understanding of Indonesian nationalism as a shared enterprise between the native Indonesians and the Dutch. Together, the two groups created a national identity for the country that was more modern, oriented to technological progress, and outward-looking. Asphalt roads were built following an increase in Dutch concerns about intermingling with the native population. An influential Dutch pharmacist warned against infection. The technology of asphalt would lift drivers out of the fetid muck of the natural terrain. Mrázek describes the colonial view of the land and its inhabitants this way: "Natives ... were speaking and writing flesh and blood, or simply mud. Wherever the natives went, and especially as they dared to approach a modern road, they were read and pronounced as carrying that soft stuff on themselves, on their tongues, on their feet, and on their wheels" (2002, 27).

Roads and other technologies were to provide a buffer between native and colonizer. What neither recognized was the essentially modernizing effect of the road which, once established, became understood by both groups as a movement toward modernity and, by extension, in support of an emerging national identity. The technologies of radio and road were developed as part of the industrial and cultural infrastructure by which the colony was governed. Eventually, with the emergence of regional cultural forms such as kroncong, technology in Indonesia was to become a kind of cultural wedge between the Dutch and the native Indonesians, thereby indirectly encouraging the development of a distinct nationalist native-Indonesian culture.

Technology and the Invention of Tradition

The earliest study of the relationship between technology and nationalism was that of the US sociologist Karl Deutsch (1966), who argued that communications technologies (the printing press, newspaper, telegraph, radio, television) supported the establishment of nationalist movements by allowing for the convenient and frequent exchange of ideas within a geographical area. Technology and nationalism in this view were brought together through culture. Before the spread of the printing press and subsequent media innovations, cultural sharing occurred only in small groups. The oral traditions of speaking, singing, and, for people with basic education, writing and reading, were used to pass a cultural heritage from one generation to the next. With the advent of technologies such as books, newspaper, radio, and television, the enduring preferences, values, and habits of culture were circulated more intensively within an emerging nation. Deutsch's cultural argument for the varying consequences for societies of different media was built on the earlier economic work of Innis (1951), which drew historical conclusions from the "bias" of a communication medium to either space or time. The conception of space and time as a phenomenon mediated by technology has profound implications for the genesis and extension of nationalist projects. However, unlike Innis, Deutsch did not give attention to differences among technologies and their varying capacities for social structuring. Instead, as Deibert notes, Deutsch was concerned with communication flows and their determination of the level of national and international integration: "Concentrated clusters of communication patterns – measured in terms of the density and flow of portal or telephone exchanges, for example – distinguish separate communities. The unevenness of this distribution helps explain why nationalism is prevalent in world politics. The flip side of this equation – and the explanation for integration, according to Deutsch – is that the density of the flow determines the scope of the community. As flows increase, parochialism dissolves" (Deibert 1997, 20).

Deutsch sought evidence for his argument in three ways. First, he used social-psychological indicators to measure the degree to which one medium functioned in tandem with another in a complementary fashion to allow for the gathering and passing on of values, preferences, and memories. Second, he measured the rate by which minority groups blended within a mainstream culture, hypothesizing that this rate depended on information about experiences exchanged within elite groups and then disseminated to the larger population. Third, he established rates of social mobility by measuring shifts from rural occupations to urban ones. Deutsch suggested that, in some cases, the use of communications technologies led to diverging cultural preferences and separate national cultures.

Following the same modernist approach to nationalism as Deutsch, B. Anderson (1996) argued that the technology of the printing press and the rise of the newspaper allowed for the development of "imagined communities." These communities were larger and more diverse than those that existed before the printing press. Before the printing press, communities were bounded by the face-to-face transmission of narratives and other forms of cultural knowledge. An individual's memory limited the scale of a community. Thereafter, community memory could be committed to books and other printed artifacts and disseminated to a larger population. With a common language, one which replaced a wider number of dialects and language variants, the newspaper helped to create an imagined community, along with a public venue for the exchange of opinions and ideas about the status and future of the nation. The national community's membership, land base, and diversity could grow quickly.

Anderson pointed to three important artifacts by which the imagined community of the nation took place in the colonial period of the nineteenth century: census, maps, and museums. The census provided a measure of how large the imagined community was and at what rate it was increasing or decreasing in size. Members of a nation could use a number to refer to the size of the population, with implications for the potential strength of the nation in terms of economic and cultural production and of armed force. The populations of towns, cities, and other jurisdictions allowed people to keep in mind a corresponding notion of mass or size of the national group. The census also provided a metric of how much force would be needed to establish the security of the nation. In a similar way, the map allowed for imagining the space within which the nation now resided, along with the adjoining space that the nation might aspire to control. The map displayed dots depicting the emerging national group's cities, and these dots were depicted in relation to the dots of other cities of the world. The map's borders showed colonized groups that they could stake claims to national identity within a territory. Eventually, they would act on this knowledge and expel the colonizing power. Museums in colonial lands arose in part out of a move toward modern schooling by imperial powers. Archeological discoveries, monuments, and reconstructions would be a means of instruction in the history and culture for natives. These were then reproduced in textbooks, postage stamps, postcards, and so on: "Interlinked with one another, then, the census, the map and the museum illuminate the late colonial state's style of thinking about its domain ... It was bounded, determinate, and therefore – in principle – countable" (B. Anderson 1996, 184).

The historical use of the census, map, and museum was not the end of the story for the development of the glory of the colonizing nation. In using the institutions of census, map, and museum to create everyday reminders of the national identity, colonizers provided the means by which native populations could develop their own "technologies of nationalism." Ironically, the colonized peoples used these institutions as the basis for developing an independent identity and as the icons of a nationalist movement.

Anderson's approach is sociological in that it seeks to account for the social structures by which nationalism is developed. It is also psychological. Anderson writes of the "two fatalities" of psychology that nationalism addresses: death and linguistic diversity (Smith 1998). The recognition or acknowledgement of death as the fate of human activity is taken up in a society through nationalism in the continuity and meaning provided through the symbolism of the national history. Linguistic diversity, reflected in the symbolism of the Tower of Babel, is addressed in the separation of nations into their linguistic groups.

Canada has the characteristics of a nationalizing state, rather than a nation-state or state-nation, because the Canadian Government is involved in continuing to shape a national identity. The nationalizing project is presentist, although its materials are historical: "Primordial verities and time-immemorial origins are re-worked by the process of re-membering the past in the present" (Osborne 2006a, 152). Memory and identity exist in a mutual relationship of influence in history, and the nationalizing state has a central role in mediating this relationship (Osborne 2002; Osborne 2006b).

Another view of the nationalizing state is Eric Hobsbawm's invention of tradition. For Gellner, nationalism makes nations. For Hobsbawm, national*ists* make nations. Central to Hobsbawm's theory of nationalism is the concept of "invented tradition." National traditions in this view are one kind of invented tradition. Custom and convention may change in response to new conditions. By contrast, an invented tradition corresponds to the past and consequently has a repetitive, invariant character: "Custom is what judges do; 'tradition' (in this instance invented tradition) is the wig, robe and other formal paraphernalia and ritualized practices surrounding their substantial action" (Hobsbawm and Ranger 1983, 2–3).

Invented traditions occur in response to the rapid change of the modern era. A "pool" of historical resources is available for the invention of tradition. Elements of tradition are retrieved, combined with other elements, and otherwise used in novel ways. An example of an invented Canadian tradition was the adoption of the maple leaf as the national emblem. While the maple leaf had been used since the nineteenth century in various provincial and even federal emblems (such as army badges, war-grave markers, and provincial flags), its official designation as part of the national flag in 1965 instantly became part of an invented tradition. The maple leaf could now have symbolic uses in the retrospective consideration of Canadian history in ways that had not previously been possible. In the ornamentation of the Parliament buildings appear representations of maple leaves that predated the new flag by several decades (Mackey 1999).

Technology, Cultural Accommodation, and the Canadian Nation-State

In Canada as elsewhere, technology limns the identity of the modern nation-state. Under the surface of technology's metallic sheen, political and cultural conflicts are accommodated, resolved, or set aside. The development of the nation-state emphasizes the role of communications using technology, as it does that of mass education, democratic and political participation, and urbanization. Technology has been the subject of discourses about social identity in Canadian history, from the railroad to radio and television broadcasting, and the internet. A special analysis of the relationship between technology and nationalism is inherent in *technological nationalism*, which refers to the rhetorical use of technology for the purpose of developing a nationalist project (Charland 1986). Technological nationalism has characterized the Canadian state's rhetoric concerning identity. Technological nationalism involves the explicit use of technology as the subject of a nationalist project's strategy. For example, technological nationalism in Canada has historically developed a set of arguments and stories referring to a national culture arising out of social process, rather than product. Charland notes that *The national dream*, a popular documentary television program of the 1980s, depicted an aboriginal confronted by a steam locomotive. The image of the railroad had become associated with the historical "national dream" of social unity to be accomplished through technological achievement. Such an achievement would be accomplished particularly through the development of communications technologies such as a transnational system of telegraph and railroad lines in the nineteenth century, a national radio and television service in the 1930s and 1940s, satellite communications in the 1970s, and, most recently, broadband internet service for remote communities. Other examples include the pipeline debate of 1956 (Pickersgill 2001), which was to be echoed in the Missile Crisis several years later, the Berger Inquiry into the proposed Mackenzie Valley Pipeline

Inquiry (1977), and, more recently, Canada's participation in the US program of developing weapons for use in space (Pugliese 2003). Technological nationalism combines the idea of technological progress with the sentiments and goals of nationalism. The state seeks legitimacy for its actions by creating, through rhetoric, a nation that mirrors its own objectives. The "bureaucracy of memory" favours elite memory over popular memory, predictable and stable public commemorations and celebrations, and historical continuity over discontinuity (Osborne 2006a, 155; Gillis 1994, 3). Technological nationalism is a view of nationalism that examines the rhetorical devices and techniques within nationalist projects for their adoption of technology as both medium and subject.

The technology of mass communications media is part of the nationalist project in both its mediating and demonstrational uses. Television, radio, newspapers, and the internet refer to the same body of cultural content, although the social effects of these messages vary by medium. The printing press and the activity of reading were important for the creation of national cultures, for example. Reading is a solitary, reflective, and individualistic activity in which the relationship of the personal to the collective of the national culture was established (Poster 1999). Radio, by contrast, evokes the collective more than it does the individual. As McLuhan (1964) notes, radio has the capacity to revive forgotten languages and bring to mind the lost glories of the nation.

Technology for some historians and sociologists is a cause or antecedent of nationalism, but for others it is an effect or outcome. The *technology as cause* approach suggests that by creating conditions that favour the development of a recognizable national identity, technology enables nationalism to take root. For example, B. Anderson (1996) describes the means by which the standardization of a national language following the use of the printing press, and in particular the medium of the newspaper, enabled communities to consolidate their national identity. Using the common language and public forum created by the newspaper, a larger, national community could coordinate economic activities that then supported and helped extend nationalist projects. Technology in this way can be a necessary antecedent of nationalism.

For other scholars, technology is an outcome or effect of a nationalist movement. Technological innovation is deployed and exploited in order to show what social and economic benefits may flow from the nationalist project. The *technology as effect* approach is based on the assumption that nationalist sentiments and energies already exist within societies. They thrive and spread, in part by exploiting technology and fostering technological advances. This approach has been central to recent studies of Asian nationalist movements. The development of the Indonesian aircraft industry from 1976 until 1997, for example, was made possible by the nationalist rhetoric employed by influential bureaucrats, politicians, technologists, and engineers in that country (Amir 2004). This rhetoric provided legitimacy to a policy of intensive research and development and the production of sophisticated aircraft. For example, it involved the public discussion of the influential idea of "technology leapfrogging." This is the idea that a national community can pass over intermediary stages of industrial development by investing heavily in a new, technologically advanced area of research, development, and production.

Causal explanations of how national identity is established, developed, and disseminated must increasingly take account of the social and psychological changes introduced by the widespread use of the internet. Many people now experience what the historian Mark Poster has called a "profound bond with machines" (Poster 1999). This bond obscures the cause-effect relationship between technology and social movements such as nationalism. The continuous and intensive exchange of ideas has created a new environment in which technology may be considered both a cause *and* an effect of nationalism. In this vein, James Carey described some four decades ago the capacity of communications media to take on a counterposing social function of this kind. In his foundational work in developing a cultural perspective on communications media, Carey (1963) distinguishes between *communication as social process* and *communication as system*. He suggests that communication as system is only one part of the picture. A complete view of communication as process reveals economic, political, and social practices that extend, abridge, mitigate, and elaborate communications media.

In the mid-twentieth century, the philosopher Grant (1965) and the historian Cook (1970) outlined the stakes for Canadian society of technological nationalism. Their contrasting conclusions on the relationship between technology and nationalism in Canada may be characterized respectively as idealist and pragmatist. They provide a means of clarifying the political issues that were in play at the time, and they remain useful for that purpose today. Taken together, the characterizations of technology and nationalism by Grant and Cook may be posed not in terms of cause and effect but as a dialectic. At certain times in the history of a nation-state and the development of a national culture, technology leads nationalism. During such a period or event – the Canadian Missile Crisis of 1962 was one and the diffusion of the networked computer in the 1990s another – nationalism is portrayed in public discussions as backward, a throwback to a premodern or agrarian predicament. It is depicted as leading to a lower standard of living. At other times, nationalism leads technology. During these periods, such as the period of economic nationalism during the 1970s in Canada, there is a vague but unstated distrust expressed in relation to technology and to the bureaucracies that manage it. At all times, the ideological tension between technology and nationalism moves the nationalist project along the path of modernity.

A view of technology and nationalism as existing in a dialectical relationship relies on a recognition of the ideological character of social action. Although nationalism is not in itself a unified system of ideas – the cultural contexts in which nationalism has thrived are too diverse to support such a notion – its aims are carried forward through ideology. The alternating historical process of first generating ideas, and then deploying technology in support of those ideas, requires the continuous production and circulation of symbols using communications technologies (Gouldner 1976). Ideologies give life to large-scale social movements such as nationalist projects. This is possible only through the use of the technology of mass media. For many nationalist projects, the newspaper has been the medium by which nationalist ideas have gained wide circulation. Modern nation-states have developed as a product of technologically mediated communication. Such technologies were invented in the modern era, and their subsequent use constituted the social character, aesthetic qualities, and administrative methods of modernism. Each nationalist identity is modern as it partakes of the benefits and symbols of technology. Nationalism is a cohesive set of ideas about the meaning of modernism for social identity, and modernism's meaning is fatally bound up with the belief that technology holds the promise of a better life for large groups of people. Technological innovation has frequently been used to highlight a state's influence and economic prestige in relation to other states. The nation-state is modern, competitive, and oriented to the adoption and use of technology. Technological innovation, including social innovation using technology, is the means by which the nationalist state advances along the path of modernization. Nationalism's progress can be traced by the social trajectory of certain technologies. Nationalist projects create myths of identity in order to link the modernist path on which the country embarks to a historical culture.

The Canadian experience of nationalism takes up technology as a discursive subject in a myth of identity. The modernist frame for nationalism must take into account those myths within which modernism itself is constituted. These include most prominently the myth of technology, along with the potential and realized cultural meanings of technology within the nation. George Grant and Ramsay Cook were prominent historical interpreters of the meaning of technology in relation to Canadian identity. Grant's view was that technology's ultimate use in Canada would be to achieve economic and political subordination to the US. A nationalist state in Canada would offer the promise of counteracting technology's colonizing effects. Cook's view was that nationalism in Canada threatened the political and social contract that allows for the nation's cultural diversity. Technology could be used to strengthen that diversity.

The Canadian experience of nationalism takes up technology directly. The Canadian state has been active throughout its relatively short history in adopting technology as a state project. The federal government's Community Access Program (CAP) has been an effort to, in the program's words, "provide Canadians with affordable public access to the Internet and the skills they need to use it effectively" (Government of Canada 2006). CAP has supported some ten thousand public access computer terminals, mainly by providing funds to libraries and schools to purchase equipment. As a consequence of the program, it is now possible to gain access to the internet in many public places in Canada. The federal government also published the report of the National Broadband Task Force (Government of Canada 2002). The report called for a national strategy for ensuring that broadband (the "big pipe" of internet access) services will be available in a consistent manner to all Canadians through the connection of public learning institutions, public health-care facilities, public libraries, and other designated public-access points.

While the social, cultural, and economic implications of the widespread and intensive use of ICTs (our ubiquitous information and communications technologies such as the mobile telephone and digital music player) are only vaguely understood (Dutton 1996; Ciborra 1996; Dutton 1999), the broadest significance of these technologies lies in their ambiguous meanings. ICTs hold the promise of new conceptions of community and a more democratized public sphere (De Kerckhove 1997; Poster 1999; Etzioni and Etzioni 1999) while simultaneously enacting a substantive basis for centralized social control (Beniger 1986). Technology, particularly communications technology, provides a rich entry into inquiries about national autonomy and its expression in cultural identity and the political expression of nationalism (Watkins 1966; Nelles and Rotstein 1973; Gagne 1976; Kroker 1984). Technology reflects at once the nationalist concerns of culture and of capital (Charland 1986). In broadcasting and communications enterprises, technology is a carrier of cultural information in the form of television shows, radio broadcasts, and so on. It is also a structuring influence in regional, national, and international economies, creating and changing patterns of trade and development in its wake (Mosco 1979; Smythe 1981; Mosco 1996). As Innis (1951) notes, culture and power exist historically in a mutual relationship of development: "The capacity to concentrate on intense cultural activity during a short period of time and to mobilize intellectual resources over a vast territory assumes to an important extent the development of armed force to a high state of efficiency" (133).

The Canadian Missile Crisis, or Defence Crisis as it has also been called, of 1962 highlighted the relationship between the act of importing foreign technology and the social, cultural, and economic goals of an autonomous Canadian nation, especially as that autonomy could be defined in contrast with that of the US (Hodgins 1973). In that historical moment, the interests associated with technology, along with its consequences and alternative choices, were exposed with some clarity. The events of 1962 are relevant for a consideration of contemporary events, because the Missile Crisis represents an episode of awakening, a point in Canadian history in which technology became a subject of public discussion in a way that it had not been previously. Canadian philosophers of technology in the decades following would expand the discursive space opened by these events. McLuhan (1964), Kroker (1984), Charland (1986), Powe (1993), and Mosco (1996) were to establish their critiques of communications technologies in the recognition, born of the Missile Crisis, that technology had developed in Canada in a historical context that had been shaped by the country's economic and military dependency.

Grant sought timeless principles of how we should live. The timelessness of Grant's ideals were in response to what Kern (1983) calls an "assault on a universal, unchanging, and irreversible public time," which he describes as a "metaphysical foundation of a broad cultural challenge to traditional notions about the nature of the world and man's place in it" (314). Grant's conception of the relationship of technology to nationalism was idealist in that he felt that Canada should pursue the goal of a just society and that non-technological principles were needed to help us shape technology's development. Without such principles, we would be drawn into the production of progressively more powerful means of doing things without the guidance as to what the means were to be used for. In his analysis of the work of Grant, McLuhan, and Innis, Kroker sees Grant as the technological pessimist: "[W]hile Grant is a tragic philosopher to McLuhan's happy rhetorician, Innis always remained a political economist of the blood" (Kroker 1984, 15–16).

In the rest of this chapter, it will be shown that both Grant and Cook were concerned about the prospects of technology's historical interrelationship with nationalism. Grant took an idealist's view of that relationship, seeing in technology the willful overpowering of nationalism. For Grant, truth existed outside of time. As Kroker puts it, "Grant's nationalism is emancipatory, a critical defence of 'local cultures' and a scatological critique of capitalism as the deep moral rot of modern society" (1984, 33). Grant's approach to technology was less pessimistic than it was principled. Grant attempted to set technology within a philosophical framework in which the pursuit of the good would trump technological innovation.

The 1962 debate concerning technology followed others, including the railway debates of the late nineteenth and early twentieth centuries (Innis 1972; MacKay 1992), the telephone debates of the 1920s and 1930s (Peers 1969), and, of particular relevance, two Royal Commissions in the 1950s. The Royal Commissions had addressed in part the emerging role of broadcasting in the development of national identity. The Massey-Lévesque Commission of 1949–51 on national development and the arts and the Fowler Commission of 1957 on broadcasting were to have significant effects on national cultural policy. However, these studies did not stir the public imagination and a level of public concern comparable to that ensuing from the Missile Crisis. The Missile Crisis ultimately engaged the US president's defence policy and has been generally regarded as contributing to a Canadian prime minister's electoral defeat. As a public event, it was a significant theme in two bestselling books in Canada – Peter C. Newman's *Renegade in power* and George Grant's *Lament for a nation: The death of Canadian nationalism*.

The views of two social and political critics of the time may be examined in an effort to develop a fertile context for a more contemporary consideration of technology and Canadian nationalism. Responding to the events of the Missile Crisis, Grant condemned technology because it carried the risk of increasing cultural homogeneity. His evaluation of technology was that it was disruptive of human efforts to understand and actualize the revelations of philosophy and religion. Cook, on the other hand, claimed that the expansion and importation of technology could be justified according to the goal of achieving equality in society by advancing through stages of industrialism. For Cook, technology was defined by the potential it represented for incremental improvements in living conditions and for its social resilience, in that it cannot be indefinitely restrained without political repression. It is argued here that although Cook's view has substantially guided Canadian policy and even individual attitudes concerning technology adoption, there are significant questions raised by the Missile Crisis that remain unexamined. In order to address these latent questions we may usefully revive the work of George Grant.

George Grant, the Missile Crisis, and the Historical Reading of Technology

Mel Hurtig, Dennis Lee, and others who publicly promoted Canadian nationalism during the 1960s and 1970s were to point to George Grant's work – and especially his book *Lament for a nation* (1965) – as their starting point for a growing recognition of the need for political action to support Canadian autonomy and cultural development. Grant's ideas were derived in significant part from Christian theology and the philosophy of Plato. Grant did not want to give up the ancient philosophical belief that values and truth were, even if subject to scrutiny and debate, essentially *revealed*, that truth and value existed outside of history. He wanted to explore that "revelation" while at the same time recognizing that history was a daily accomplishment and that the horizon of social development was constantly changing and ultimately unknowable (Grant 1969). Martin Heidegger's philosophical hermeneutics was for Grant a means through which the timeless truths and values of the world could be viewed. Heidegger's conception of being-in-the-world was founded on a belief in the irreducibility of natural experience and of the primacy of words and language for understanding human experience (Heidegger 1962). Grant's intellectual influences also included, by way of Heidegger, the philosophy of Friedrich Nietzsche. Grant found much to admire in Nietzsche's claim that Western society faced a crisis in the decline of the influence of Greek philosophy and Christianity (Kroker 2004, Nietzsche 2001). The claim by Nietzsche that an ethos of nihilism characterized modern society, and his sympathetic view of Christ but not of Christianity (Nietzsche 2005), were taken up by Grant in his own social critique.

Grant was born in Toronto in 1918, attending Upper Canada College as a youth and then studying at Queen's University and later Oxford University, completing a D.Phil. in theology in 1950. His working life was spent mainly as a university teacher at McMaster and Dalhousie Universities, although he had worked as a young man on the London docks in Bermondsey during the Battle of Britain, on a farm in Buckinghamshire, and as the national secretary of the Canadian Association for Adult Education (Faris 1975). It was while teaching at McMaster University that Grant initiated a public discussion about fundamental questions about Canadian identity and the Canadian nation-state. The event that gave rise to this discussion took place in 1962 and concerned the most sophisticated and powerful applications of technology: nuclear arms. What became known as the Missile Crisis in Canada directed a spotlight to the relationship between the promise of an autonomous Canadian nation and the potential threat Grant believed was inherent in the importation of technology. *Lament for a nation* was written as a response to this historical event, which figures prominently in its pages.

Beginning in 1961, the Canadian federal government under Prime Minister John Diefenbaker had authorized the installation of land-based anti-aircraft weapons, called Bomarc missiles, at sites in Ontario and Québec. Canada was participating in a joint program of defence, a plan that provided for the arming and, under certain circumstances, the use of nuclear weapons. The Bomarcs would eventually be armed with nuclear warheads, a final and necessary step if the missiles were ever to be used. The Canadian deployment of Bomarc missiles was driven by the US military buildup – and in particular a dramatically expanding missile-production program – that had begun after World War II but which reached its apex of activity during the early 1960s. The launch of the Sputnik satellite by the USSR in October 1957 had symbolic importance for its demonstration of the technological achievement of the USSR. It raised US fears that the "missile gap," which was the difference in the number and pace of production of missiles between the two countries, represented first-strike capability for the USSR, to which the US could not effectively respond. Although some analysts dispute that a missile gap actually existed (see, for example, Ball 1980), the issue nonetheless became a factor in the 1960 presidential election in the US and led to Senator Kennedy committing to an increase in military expenditures that would emphasize a speedup in the production and deployment of ballistic missiles. During the election campaign Kennedy "projected the theme that the United States had suffered an unnecessary slowing of progress under Eisenhower … He spoke positively and without equivocation as early as 23 January 1960, when he said that the United States had become 'second in space – second in missiles'" (Ball 1980, 16). After the US election a momentum developed for missile production and deployment, which extended to the period of the Cuban Missile Crisis: "After entering office, the Kennedy Administration undertook the largest and fastest peacetime military buildup in the history of the United States. The results were striking. Although the 'missile gap' had apparently been a significant factor in the 1960 election, by late 1961 members of the Kennedy Administration had publicly announced that it no longer existed" (Beard 1976, 213).

The Cuban Missile Crisis in which Canada became caught up followed a fundamental reorganization of administrative and technical control of the US military. By the end of 1960, the US had redeveloped its revised nuclear-war strategies, which now emphasized redesigning the powerful Minuteman missiles, as well as a refitting of the command and control system. Some basic figures illustrate the massive scale of the increases in missile program activities that characterized the time. Ten years earlier, in 1951, the US had spent only $500,000 annually on intermediate-range and intercontinental ballistic missiles (IR/ICBMS). By 1961, the annual amount was $3.424 billion. Total spending on missiles of all kind, including aircraft-launched missiles, had increased exponentially during this period, but IR/ICBMS occupied an increasingly dominant part of that spending. Spending on these as a proportion of total missile programs during the decade increased from .06 percent to 50 percent. The IR/ICBM portion of missile spending had therefore increased by some eight hundred times during the decade (Beard 1976, 206).

On 22 October 1962, in response to a perceived buildup of Soviet weapons in Cuba, President Kennedy requested that Canadian defence forces adopt a state of heightened readiness. Permission to station US jets in Canada and to move nuclear warheads to Newfoundland from Maine was part of the request. The prime minister balked. Peter C. Newman, a journalist and prominent analyst of the Diefenbaker years, writes that the day after the request was made by the US president, "Cabinet met … with most of the ministers feeling that endorsement of the American move would be nothing more than a formality. But the mood around the Privy Council table changed when [External Affairs Secretary] Howard Green delivered what was the most impassioned appeal of his political life. He pleaded that reconsideration be given to the idea of blindly following the United States lead … 'If we go along with the Americans now,' he said, 'we'll be their vassals forever'" (Newman 1973, 337).

On 24 October, Kennedy demanded that Cuba remove its missiles and imposed a blockade. At about 1 PM that day, the Canadian units of NORAD had assumed, forty-two hours after being asked to do so, the state of readiness requested by the US. The delay became a source of bitter political criticism and of the eventual defeat of Diefenbaker at the polls the following year. On 24 January 1963, Diefenbaker spoke in Parliament about the "preponderant" power of the US in the world, implying that the Canadian military position could at times be different than the one specified by the US. On 25 February 1963, Diefenbaker dissolved Parliament. Grant notes that during Diefenbaker's speech in Parliament that day, the prime minister "made clear that the one thing he would not stomach was the United States government determining Canadian defence policy" (Grant 1965, 30). In the ensuing federal election, Diefenbaker was defeated by Lester Pearson, who promised to take a more cooperative attitude with the US on defence issues.

The reasons for Diefenbaker's hesitation to deploy the Bomarcs have been disputed over the years. Some observers – Newman was one – reduced the event to a mere symptom of Diefenbaker's personal tendency to dither. Grant, by contrast, felt the act was part of the prime minister's larger determination to maintain Canada's sovereignty and national autonomy. However, no one disputes the significance of the Canadian Government's decision to refuse to agree immediately and without meaningful reflection to US-led military action. The nuclear warheads had become symbols of technology in an event whose meanings became entwined with the question of Canadian self-determination. Grant argued that, with the defeat of Diefenbaker's government in 1963, Canadian nationalism was now finished. If an autonomous Canada had once been possible, the events of 1962 and 1963 sealed Canadian nationalism's defeat. Referring to the Missile Crisis, Grant observes that, "[Diefenbaker's] nationalism occasioned the strongest stand against satellite status that any Canadian government ever attempted. He maintained his stand even when the full power of the Canadian ruling class, the American government, and the military were brought against him ... Diefenbaker saw his destiny as revivifying the Canadian nation" (1965, 12). Grant's view was that the Missile Crisis provided evidence that Diefenbaker's nationalism was sincere, that the only explanation for Diefenbaker to have enjoined the crisis was that he was convinced of its symbolic and substantive importance in relation to Canadian national autonomy: "The Defence Crisis of 1962 and 1963 revealed the depth of Diefenbaker's nationalism. Except for these events, one might interpret him as a romantic demagogue yearning for recognition...The government of the United States should not be allowed to force the Canadian government to a particular defense policy. His determination to stand on that belief finally convinced the ruling class that he was more than a nuisance, that he must be removed" (Grant 1965, 25).

What was the relationship between the Missile Crisis and Grant's developing conception of technology and its relationship to national culture and identity? Although the theme was not developed directly in *Lament for a nation*, the French philosopher Jacques Ellul's conception of technology figured prominently in Grant's later work (Grant 1969 and 1986) and existed in a nascent form in *Lament for a nation*. Ellul defined technology as a broadly encompassing set of social practices. He used the term *technique* to distinguish this totalizing aspect of technology. He argued that technique had a deterministic character and that it had escaped the power of people to influence its direction. In comparing science and technique, Ellul states that technique is "autonomous and recognizes as barriers only the temporary limits of its action" (1967, 142). Ellul describes the example of fish in the depths of the ocean to illustrate the distinction. He notes that "science" would seek to observe a school of fish, compare new evidence with old, photograph, and thereby seek to understand it better. Technique, by contrast, "captures them, hauls them up to see if they are edible – but before they arrive on deck they burst" (142). For Ellul, technology would eventually remove from human life any mystery or risk:

Technique advocates the entire remaking of life and its framework, because they have been badly made. Since heredity is full of chance, technique proposes to suppress it so as to engender the kind of men necessary for its ideal of service. The creation of the ideal man will soon be a simple technical operation. It is no longer necessary to rely on the chances of the family or on the personal vigor which is called virtue. Applied biogenetics is an obvious point at which technique desacralizes, but we must not forget psychoanalysis, which holds that dreams, visions, and the psychic life in general are nothing more than objects. (Ellul 1967, 142–3)

In *Lament for a nation,* Grant set the stage for the fertile idea he would develop further in his later work – that technology could not be viewed as an instrument of a particular society. It was a phenomenon that must be regarded in terms of its cumulative effects across societies. For Ellul/Grant, technology had a totalizing influence on all cultures generally, changing the trajectory of human evolution and the physical environment: "The practical question is whether a society in which technology must be oriented to cybernetics can maintain the institutions of free politics and the protection by law of the rights of the individual" (Grant 1985, 10).

For both Ellul and Grant, choices about technology were made on the basis of "one best method," but the measurement to determine the best method was a narrow market-based system of prices. The best method was the one that cost the least in a market in which actors made single transactions that were divorced from the social context in which they occurred. From this perspective, technology would eventually dissolve any cultural distinctiveness that Canada could claim, leaving a homogenous, technologically driven but morally hollow society in North America and eventually the world. This evaluation may be compared with the Innisian view of the social uses of technology. For Innis, a society's primary technology represented an imbalance of power within the society and in relation to other societies. Technological biases were for Innis the blindspots that conceivably held the key to understanding particular societies and empires. Members of a society in which writing was the primary technology were oblivious to important aspects of seeing and experiencing the world. Members of societies in which orality held sway would be oblivious in ways that were categorically different from perceptions associated with a culture in which writing was dominant. Both Grant and Innis therefore saw communications technologies as having two potential effects: either extending an empire or nurturing a local or regional culture. Innis's time-space conception, which Grant took up as "time as history" versus

Plato's "time as the moving image of eternity," is expressed by Carey in his comment on the diverging meanings of communication as transmission and as ritual: "If the archetypal case of communication under a transmission view is the extension of messages across geography for the purpose of control, the archetypal case under a ritual view is the sacred ceremony that draws persons together in fellowship and commonality" (Carey 1989, 18).

In his later writings, Grant frequently reminds his readers that important questions raised by technology were only dimly understood: "The practical question is whether a society in which technology must be oriented to cybernetics can maintain the institutions of free politics and the protection by law of the rights of the individual" (1985, 10). The case of Canada's autonomy was an extension of an ancient dialogue about how people ought to live (Grant 1969). Technology had escaped from the restraints of philosophy and religion by means of a new society in North America whose exploits were motivated by the tenets of Calvinist Christianity. The Protestant work ethic described by sociologist Max Weber (1930) was characterized by the belief in earthly striving for material success and wealth, which could be considered a sign of providential blessing. For Grant, a philosopher with a deep knowledge of theology, Christianity and the ancient Greek philosophers had together established a moral code for society that had been severed from the experience of North America in the effort to create a society of equals and in order to tame or master nature. In Grant's account, technological development constituted the single modern worldview, considered by both Marxists and liberals as the means by which a society of equal citizens could be created. Technology was the "dominant morality," he explained, and as a result most people could not evaluate its effects critically. A moral haze had settled on North America, and its source was the smokestack of state capitalism: "Leisure is only possible with the division of labour. But the division of labour without modern mastery resulted in inequality – particularly the grossest inequality in leisure. The noblest expectation of the age of progress was to overcome that limitation by building a society in which all men would come to have leisure through the mastery that science would make possible" (Grant 1969, 129).

For Grant, the expansion of US political and military influence in the world was enabled and driven by the expansion and elaboration of technology. Canadian nationalism was not to be feared, because it carried the promise of a reversal of empire and a return to the hope for a society in which contemplation of the good would be made possible. Grant the philosopher was not specifically concerned with the historically demonstrable dangers of nationalism. History was the mode in which the contemplative achievements of Athens and Jerusalem were revealed. History had to be viewed in much broader terms than were considered by the proponents of one military policy or another.

With the publication of *Lament for a nation*, some claimed that Grant was mourning the death of conservatism in Canada – conservatism as a social force or perhaps as a political party. Grant denied this, and it should be remembered that in 1960, on the eve of the Missile Crisis, he contributed "An ethic of community" to *Social purpose for Canada*, a book published in concert with the founding of the New Democratic Party. His political leanings were tied less to particular political ideologies than to philosophical ideals. Grant felt that the embrace of technology implied a disregard for the moral frame within which human action must be assessed: "[T]he truth of natural law is that man lives within an order which he did not make and to which he must subordinate his actions; the truth of the history-making spirit is that man is free to build a society which eliminates the evils of the world. Both these assertions seem true. The difficulty is to understand how they both can be brought together" (1960, 89–90).

Defence, technology, and corporate expansionism: for Grant, these were interlaced components that dissolved local cultures. Canada's culture, which was always under threat as a consequence, first by British imperialism and then by the US, could not withstand the levelling effects of technology. Grant believed that, over time, the adoption of foreign technology would degrade Canada's autonomy. His views on technology formed a central part of his mature scholarly work. His *Technology and empire*, published a few years after *Lament for a nation*, argued that imperialism and conquest were conjoined with the instrumental uses of technology (Grant 1969). He became increasingly persuaded by the Ellulian conception of technology less as a complement of hardware and software than as a totalizing set of social practices.

Grant called for a nationalism that would delineate Canada's identity as an independent country whose view of the world would contrast with the US view more than it would complement it.

Ramsay Cook, the Missile Crisis, and the Historical Reading of Nationalism

Ramsay Cook, then a professor of history at York University, read *Lament for a nation* and responded to the book's main claims in a 1970 article published in the *Journal of Canadian Studies*. In the article, Cook explained Grant's views in part on the basis of personal background. He pointed out that Grant was the grandson of Principal G.M. Grant and Sir George Parkin, "liberal Christians who identified the progress of mankind with the preservation and spread of Anglo-Saxon civilization" (Cook 1970, 51). The personal and biographical were part of Cook's analysis, although it must be stated that human equality was a core value of Grant's: "I have no doubt that within Christianity everyone is equal before God ... ultimately, before God, people are equal" (Grant, quoted in Cayley 1995, 58).

Cook correctly identified within *Lament for a nation* the key concern of technology and its fundamental character, a concern that Grant would indeed expand in his later writing. Significantly, in the intervening half-decade since the appearance of *Lament for a nation*, Grant had published *Technology and empire*, which more explicitly linked the expansion of US influence throughout the world with US elaboration and deployment of technology internationally. Cook notes in the article that, although Grant had earlier in his life believed that technology should be used to relieve the hardships of daily life for the masses, his later work would describe technology as having a deterministic character. He describes Grant's assumptions as follows: "[T]he age of technology, with its liberal ideology and its commitment to progress, was the age of the 'universal and homogeneous state.' By definition particular cultures and nations were doomed to disappear" (Cook 1970, 56).

For his part, Cook felt it was reasonable to accept the risks of importing and developing technology, which could be the loss of some national autonomy, while rejecting the risks of nationalism, which could be anomie and crisis and which he felt to be much greater threats. History was a daily accomplishment of actors and groups of actors in Cook's worldview, and no essential or revealed lessons from the past could be admitted. Contingent caution as regarded technology could be advanced based on knowledge of the past. Technology was what we would decide it would be, and Canada would remain autonomous if it had the political will to do so.

For Cook the historian, nationalism as a political or social movement was something to be skeptical about, to be viewed with more scrutiny than was technology. Born in Saskatchewan in 1931, Cook was to publish on political and constitutional history in the 1970s and 1980s, on English-French relations, intellectual and artistic life, and, in the latter part of his career, exploration and European contact with native North Americans. Technology is not a central concern in Cook's writing – at that time or since – although a consideration of the relationship of history to the environment became a theme of his work in the 1990s (Cook 1993). As a student of Canadian federal development, Cook saw nationalism in English Canada as a threat to whatever social balance had been carefully achieved with French Canada. The question for him was not, "If nationalism?" but, "If nationalism, which one?" Nationalism was a set of ideas that inevitably led economic and political action, and such action might just sweep away the accomplishments of Canadian federalism. Nationalism, not technology, was the concept requiring a full conceptual analysis for a view of the largest dangers. Political determination or will could have violent consequences when exercised by nationalists. Political action initiated by the state was still an important fact in the world and something that should not be discounted in comparisons with technology: "[T]he Canadian nation state, a non-nationalist state, is worthy of preservation. It provides the frame in which thinking can take place, values be reassessed, and action taken" (Cook 1970, 59).

So there was common ground between Cook and Grant. Both believed technology could undermine nationalism. The difference was that Grant contemplated this with sorrow, while Cook welcomed it. Writing about the same question twenty-five years later, Cook had not changed his opinion. He states that through the window of nationalism could be viewed the horrors of nineteenth-century European warfare: "History shows that . . . 'ideologists' are always milder than the practical politicians who follow in their footsteps" (Cook 1995, 18). For Cook, nationalism would be properly, and only, the striving for self-determination. Self-determination was a worthy goal but one that should find its achievement in political compromises, not in the philosophical rejection of technology based on a historical view: "Nationalism is often expressed in the evangelistic rhetoric of a secular religion, offering redemption and salvation to sinners. But like other missionary religions, nationalism has never solved the problem of the backslider, how to keep the flock true to the faith. This world's temptations or necessities are too demanding, promise of a 'new man' and a 'new society' too ethereal" (Cook 1995, 18).

It should be noted that technology, too, may be constituted through social discourse in religious terms (Noble 1999) or as part of a body of social myths (Romanyshyn 2004). In any event, cultural diversity within Canada was for Cook a fact expressed in the political arrangements made for Québec within confederation – and which could be contrasted with what Cook called Grant's "Anglo-Saxon civilization." Creating a nationalist state would isolate Canada, but such isolation would in the end be impossible given Canada's cultural diversity and democratic values. A nationalist Canadian state, one isolated by a rejection or avoidance of technological advances, would not be compatible with the political balance found in Canadian federalism. Cook's notion of incremental federalism had a counterpart in incremental technological advance. In the same way that relations between the federal government and the provinces could always be changed and were actually always in flux, so, too, changes in the uses and applications of technology were bound to occur. Technology was not an entity with relatively fixed characteristics, but one that could always be made subject to human will, in this case the further development of Canadian federalism. The question, of course, is whose will and for what purpose.

On one side of the dialectic, then, technology was regarded with caution by Grant because it carried the risk of further cultural homogeneity. With US "know-how," the argument went, came US "willhow." The importation of technology was not a neutral phenomenon, but one that carried with it the machinery of imperialism. Grant tended to examine technology with a more disciplined eye than he did nationalism – a historian's eye rather than a philosopher's. Cook, on the other hand, was more interested in *nationalism* as a historical phenomenon, or process, than in looking at technology in the same way (Cook 1966, 1995). Cook claimed that the expansion and importation of technology could be justified in light of the goal of achieving equality in society by advancing through stages of industrialism. For him, it was not necessary to define the conception of technology in the way that Grant had relied on Ellul to do. It was enough to conclude that the practical application of Grant's views would lead to an industrially and culturally isolated Canada. Technology could be defined adequately as, for example, the means by which the environment could be protected: "[D]espite Grant and Ellul, the evidence suggests some small reason for accepting the view that technological change need not determine political decisions, but rather that political decisions can direct and limit technological development. The control of pollution is an obvious example of what should be done and what must be done" (Cook 1970, 59).

The pervasiveness of pollution in the first place was a consequence, using Grant's critique, of the unprincipled adoption of technology. The common ground between Grant and Cook should therefore be underlined. Both saw technology as requiring well-considered social and political underpinnings; both sought self-determinative powers for the Canadian state. Grant's radical conservatism had as its object a more deeply philosophical approach to the development and adoption of technology. He was opposed to an unquestioning acceptance of what Ursula Franklin (1992) was to call "prescriptive technologies" and in relation to which Grant called for a return to the Platonic notion of separating "making" (the Greek *techne*) from "knowing" (*logos*). Davis (1996) observes that for Grant, "[a] new form of knowing (and producing) things had emerged, which assumed a change in our relation to nature and to God. Grant accepted Heidegger's help on this, as he had earlier accepted the help of Ellul and others" (144). We are to be measured by timeless truth and values, Grant claimed, but when we set out to define these truths and values through the "will to technology," all creation suffers the consequences.

The political effect of Grant's ideas was to spur an explicit Canadian nationalism, which was taken up by cultural and economic national-ists in the 1960s and 1970s. Jill Vickers describes these ideas as a package that "linked anti-modernism, anti-Americanism, technological de-terminism and an almost unthinking reliance on the state" (1994). Just as Cook argued in 1970 that pollution of the environment provided an urgent example of an instance in which technology had a positive role to play, Vickers argued some twenty-five years later that the status of women had benefited from the application of technology and could benefit further. In any case, technology was not the only or even the most important influence on cultural development: "[T]he anti-mod-ernist attribution of profound identity changes resulting in cultural homogenization to the effects of modern technology alone betrays a framework ignorant of the roles of women as they craft and transmit language and identity even in the face of massive oppression and intru-sion" (Vickers 1994, 366).

Technology, for Cook and for Vickers, is not a dynamo, devouring and levelling cultures, but a tool for gradually improving daily life. In this sense, the difference between Grant's idealism and Cook's prag-matism is not resolvable on its face. To consider the case of the internet, for example, there are undeniable benefits to individuals and groups as a consequence of the implementation of these technologies, but it must be noted as well that these benefits are distributed unevenly and that ultimate outcomes are not known in advance.

Conclusion: The Fate of the Grant-Cook Dialectic

Alternating within a dialectic of idealism and pragmatism regarding the widespread use of the internet, between forms of pessimism and optimism, may be the most appropriate approach to ensuring that historical readings of both technology and nationalism are incorporated in a social, cultural, and economic process of development in Canada. In the same way that the missiles arrived in Québec, the internet sta-tions have arrived in homes and workplaces. By considering a parallel historical case that suggests something of the "disturbance" that is possible and even desirable, the Grant-Cook dialectic may help us to see more clearly the urgency of mindfully assessing the uses and purposes of technology.

A contemporary view of technology set within the Missile Crisis discourse would acknowledge the ideological nature of the technological-nationalist discourse. Ideologies are developed as individuals and groups seek broadly encompassing accounts of how their interests may be protected and advanced (Gellner 1965 and 1994). Ideology supports the actions of individuals and groups in those instances in which the legitimacy of these actions is challenged. In this way, state action is legitimated and implicitly or explicitly approved by most members of the polity. After Mr Diefenbaker raised the question of whether the missiles could be stationed on Canadian soil without a substantive decision in Canada on the matter, an ideological account of state action was required. The contributions of Grant and Cook helped create the disturbance that has been set out here. Yet no such disturbance is associated with contemporary adoptions of technology. It is in this sense that the social landscape is categorically different than it was in 1962. The rejection by Prime Minister Diefenbaker of nuclear warheads was met by a strong reaction, both for and against. The disturbance of the Missile Crisis led to a change in government and the rise of a new nationalist movement in Canada. Yet there followed little public debate in the following decades. For example, the plan by Prime Minister Trudeau in the 1980s to test cruise missiles in Canada's north was met by only mild opposition. The tests were carried out, thereby allowing for the missiles' deployment and use by the US in attacks in the following decade on Iraq and the former Yugoslavia.

What disturbances there are more recently in Canada – the debate about continued troop deployment in Afghanistan, for example – have yet to lead to a significant shift in how Canadians regard the larger implications of technological development that Grant described. Since the Missile Crisis, Canada's participation in the use of technology for both peaceful and non-peaceful purposes (Cook's "temptations or necessities" that lead technological innovation) has increased dramatically. The historical argument against nationalism has evidently been the more influential as regards technology. Indeed, when Cook warned against a nationalist state, he was supporting what can be assumed to be the opinion of the majority of Canadians. This majority wishes the state to be largely invisible as regards the interactions of technology and nationalism. The state in Canada retains the appearance of public neutrality as regards the importation of technology. Of course, states uphold laws that are not neutral in their enactment and amendment, favouring instead some groups rather than others. However, the appearance of neutrality is maintained in the enforcement of law. To the extent that a nationalist identity exists in Canada, it is to be based on the confederal purpose of maintaining the country's cultural and political variation. Canadians generally hold a historical, pragmatic reading of nationalism and have largely rejected nationalism as a legitimate movement or way of thinking. The spectre of the ongoing and bloody conflicts in Eastern Europe have provided a useful moral instructive for cautioning against the excesses of ethnocentrism and even the mildest expressions of nationalism. The historical reading of technology advocated by Grant, on the other hand, has neither been accepted nor rejected, only set aside as potentially disruptive to political, social, and economic life in Canada. Certain risks are accepted whenever a new technology is adopted, but individuals, groups, and nations must be mindful of the existence of these risks if informed decisions are to be made about accepting or not accepting such risks.

Grant worked out his views on the basis that technology would determine social structure by stunting a nascent cultural identity. Cook argued the reverse, that social structures could and should shape the development of technology. A dialectical approach, in sympathy with the perspective of Bruno Latour (see, for example, Latour 1996; Strum and Latour 1987), would allow for a synthesis of these positions. In this view, a mutual interaction of *actor* and *actant* (technology or other actors) occurs in which a technology is continually redefined and redescribed by actors. The authority of an actor is enhanced by the network of other actors for whom that actor speaks but also by the influence of the technologies themselves. James Taylor summarizes this view as follows: "It is nonhuman actors that both enable and constrain because they provide the means by which actions are amplified" (Taylor and Van Every 2000, 159). Latour's example of the traffic speed bump is insightful here. Once a technology is established, it continues to act and influence actors and actants, regardless of whether there is further intervention by actors. The design of the technology sets the pattern for ultimate outcomes, in this case a continuous sequence of vehicles slowing their speed. Technology "acts back" on us, even after the actors who designed and built the technology have left the scene. Unintended consequences occur because technology changes social relations, and these social relations create new frames within which unanticipated results can and do occur.

For Ellul and Grant, decisions on the adoption of technology were based on short-term considerations, when they ought to consider potential long-term consequences. It is in this sense that the possibility of redesign must be considered as a matter of social policy. Diefenbaker's critics bitterly pointed out that the Bomarcs were useless without their nuclear warheads and that Diefenbaker knew this when he had initially approved their installation. By implication, the charge was that Diefenbaker disingenuously claimed that there were two decisions associated with the missile program – one to deploy, the other to arm – when in fact there was only one. The potential for redesign – with the associated question of who may redesign – should be of prime importance as new technologies are adopted in Canada. Cook's pragmatist approach implies an open potential for redesign. This potential is inherent in the incremental changes and even retrenchment that are thought to be possible at each stage of social development. It assumes that the choices for change are always available. By contrast, Ellul/Grant would argue that technology's totalizing effects are structurally obscured from view and that redesign is not always a clear choice. The consequences of technology are often socially resilient; in some cases they cannot be rescinded. It is not simply the technologies that societies choose or do not choose but also the social outcomes with which those technologies will become historically associated.

In the 1960s, Grant and Cook developed sophisticated perspectives on Canadian nationalism. Their diverging views of the relationship of nationalism to the importation of technology has relevance for Canada in an age in which ICTs are crowding personal, corporate, and national agendas. A reconsideration of Grant's idealistic orientation to technology and Cook's pragmatic orientation provides a dialectic that can illuminate the meaning and possible effects of imported technologies for Canadians at the beginning of the millennium. Although

Grant and Cook did not debate these issues with one another in a formal setting, their opposing perspectives provide a conceptual tool for presenting and exploring richly divergent ideas and their potential application to contemporary concerns.

In raising again the dormant issues raised by Grant and Cook concerning nationalism's relationship to the importation of technology to Canada it must be noted that the contemporary situation differs from that of the 1960s in important ways. First, the interactions of technology with people's lives are likely to be more immediate and encompassing today than they were in 1962. The Missile Crisis carried importance for all Canadians, but only in an indirect way. Although most Canadians would be influenced by the events surrounding the crisis, the vast majority of Canadians would not participate in these events. Today, ICTs are becoming an increasingly direct part of many Canadians' experience at home and at work. The state is involved in encouraging this lived experience. The federal government, along with other institutions, such as public libraries and learning institutions, has set the priority of equalizing access to these technologies by, for example, helping to establish internet stations in public places.

Second, while in 1962 the importation of technology was for the stated purpose of enhancing national defence and security, it is now an explicit part of the effort to render Canadian citizens as fully competitive and participative international actors. In the last two decades, the changing nature of competition and a rapidly increasing level of globalization have fashioned productivity into what has been called a "creative force" of global competitiveness (Smothers 1990). ICTs are embedded in this drive for increases in productivity. Entwined with the effort to improve national productivity through the use of technology are new organizational forms that are created for the purpose of speeding up production or rationalizing previously looser labour arrangements. Canadian culture will be fatefully influenced by these technologies. The present historical moment, in which Canadians are beginning to use these technologies intensively and frequently, would be appropriate for the consideration of some likely social outcomes.

In practice, Grant's argument about the relationship between technology and nationalism – which was that Canadian autonomy was at risk in the adoption of technology – is unfortunately all but forgotten.

Canadians have become skilled developers of technology intended not only for domestic use, but, more importantly for its structuring effects, for sale to an international market. They develop pharmaceuticals on the prairies, create advanced computer software in the nation's capital, and establish call centres in the Maritimes.

What has not yet faded are the pressing questions of whether we understand the limits that technology has placed on Canada's autonomy and to what extent the adoption of (mainly US) technology is likely to continue to dissolve national cultures and in particular a distinctive Canadian culture (Dorland 1996). Contemporary discussion of the appropriate uses and applications of technologies, especially ICTs, tends to set aside questions of national identity. Grant's call for a critical approach to technology, while failing to account for technology's socially progressive uses, continues to hold the promise of helping us assess how and why Canadians should approach the issue of the adoption of new technologies.

The intellectual tradition connected to technological nationalism in Canada is, like that of the nationalist project in many countries, both modern and antimodern. On the one hand, technology use arises as part of a discourse about the status of modernity, and in particular about the role of the citizen in the national culture. Nationalism concerns itself with technology because the age of modernity is an age of technology. In Canada, technology is at the centre of a discourse about Canada's identity in a world of nations. While demonstrating the modernity of the national project, technology paradoxically mediates the tension between modernity and antimodernity through its capacity to bring forward historical texts. Grant's philosophy involved the call of an ancient tradition and of a felt historical social identity as a basis for national unity. His eloquent, antimodern apologies for the traditions of Athens and Jerusalem would not have found the audience they did without the channels, gateways, and networks of modernity.

In the next chapter, a model is presented to depict how ideas about technology emerge and are accommodated in the national culture. It will be argued that (a) technology is decisively and fatefully entwined with both regional and national identities; and (b) national identity is a discursive accomplishment between region and nation. Two important shifts from Gellner's theory of nationalism should be noted.

First, this is much more of a contextualist approach. Gellner's abstract and precise laws of nationalism have not allowed for a substantive consideration of the role of social identity and culture in their regional contexts. A contextualist approach to the analysis of nationalism may therefore use the concept of the nation as an assumed organizing principle of the national space, while recognizing that other principles are simultaneously at work. Alternative logics that can be considered include, for example, the transnationalist logic of the ownership of broadcast media, the logic of neocolonialism, or the logic of international development assistance. A contextualist approach allows for the analysis of these logics in comparison with the nationalist logic of organizing: "If one accepts, with the proponents of contextualism, that the nation is not an unproblematic, transhistorical entity, but rather a complex assemblage of flows, materials, bodies, and symbols, the terrain of debate is productively shifted towards concrete analysis, away from universal claims grounded in idealized and dehistoricized concepts of 'the nation'" (Wiley 2004, 90).

Second, the popular use of communications media implies a new subject for national identity, that of "glocalism" (Robertson 1995), something that Gellner only hinted at in his work. A new cosmopolitanism of the kind that Appiah (2006) describes is now possible – the prospect of living as "citizens of the world," but now a world of global trade and transnational cultural flows. Canadians are well-placed because of history and geography to seek new ways of recognizing the validity of group identities within the nation-state (Kymlicka 1995) and to seek alternative political practices and processes to support diverse cultural voices (Manning 2003). Canadians in this view could strive to act as members of their local and regional communities, in addition to holding citizenship in the nation-state, while being conscious of and responsive to a global community.

3

NATIONALISM AND REGIONALISM

> What remains to be seen is whether or not
> [Gellner's] reduction has been too rigorous,
> that is, whether there is not a case to be made
> for the consideration of its internal logic.
>
> van den Bossche 2003, 494

Nationalism is a modern phenomenon involving a particular material basis for its existence. That material basis is industrialization, which has certain requirements, including a dynamic occupational structure and a division of labour allowing for specialization. Gellner's modernist theory views nationalism at the macrosocial level, portraying nationalism as a consequence of global industrialization. Both nationalism and industrialization require a homogenous culture. Such a culture provides the conditions under which, in Gellner's famous phrase, the "political and the national unit should be congruent" (1983). The modern national society as a culturally unified entity ready to meet and marry its administrative state represents a *political* principle. The cultural homogenization that industrialization produced was to be found in all nation-states and did not seem to be hindered by particular cultural developments. Gellner was therefore opposed to searching for cultural factors as the *explanans* that could be identified and analyzed at the level of either the nation or the region: "[If] nationalism is a general phenomenon, covering a whole variety of nations, quite obviously it cannot be explained by the reasons operating internally within each national movement: these reasons must be specifically related to each nation and its culture; they cannot apply generally, otherwise there could hardly be rival nationalisms. So the general explanation cannot be internal to the cultures concerned: it must stand outside them" (1997, 95).

Yet a description of particular nations and the development of the nation-state must take into account the local and regional logic by which the idea of nationalism is made familiar to a population in their activities of daily life. Not all nationalist projects "succeed," and the variables underlying success are therefore of interest to students of nationalism. Furthermore, nationalism is a social process that must extend past the date on which the nation-state is founded. It involves not only the initial determination about the nation-state's founding but also the continuing activities aimed at ensuring that the coupling remains tight between the national culture and the administrative home of the state.

The modernist theory of nationalism holds that individuals come to accept a consistent and unified communication mode within a national culture, although that mode conflicts with tradition. Serious objections to the homogenized idiom are marginalized or lose their energy after a period of time. But in what ways do individuals accept this new communication mode? What can be made of their decision not to insist on traditional modes of communication? And what are the means by which their objections to the new communication mode decline in intensity and eventually fall away? These questions point to particular nationalisms and to regional histories. And they point to technology because they concern choices about the meaning of technological development. A model of a nationalist logic of organizing in regions is modern in its approach to both culture and power. It places technology at the centre of cultural development. Technology provides not only the capacity to exchange messages rapidly. It also creates a repository for cultural knowledge. Even for oral cultures, technological devices such as databases and recordings contribute to the development of a secondary orality (Ong 2002). An ethnic identity, with its immemorial myths, is simply another cultural resource or input. Technology is at all times an expression of instrumental action.

Even when it is *felt* as an authentic expression of culture, technology use involves the enactment of will.

As the Missile Crisis of 1962 illustrated, technology and nationalism rely on one another for their mutual development in national spaces. In this chapter, I argue for giving particular attention to regional cultural development in the context of technology adoption and use. To that end, a model will be proposed that describes the conditions for a nationalist logic of organizing in regions. The model may be used to explore how and in what circumstances the nationalist idea is likely to flourish and in what circumstances it is likely to lead to the political union of nation and state and its maintenance.

The next section provides a theory of social action underlying the model, one that takes into account the likelihood that nationalist organizing is not a fully conscious experience for actors. The subsequent two sections consider the ideological uses of technology in nationalist initiatives and the implications for the study of regionalism, following which *regions* is defined in the sense in which the term will be used in the model. The model of nationalist logic of organizing in regions is then presented, supported by three premises.

Culture, Language, and the Intentions of Nationalists

The *cultural* activity of creating a homogenous society is a process that involves the common language practices of individuals and groups within the society. Cultural practices represent the prescriptions and proscriptions by which social action is made possible. People take up a single national identity through the use of idiomatic expressions, in the metaphors and turns of phrase ("language games") that characterize one national context and not another. This is done more or less unconsciously, much in the manner that games are played. Players are only fully mindful of the rules of the game when a rule is breached. Even then, it is only a generalized knowledge of what the rules mean in practice that is relevant to future action. A nationalist logic of organizing may in this sense be understood in relation to Bourdieu's concept of games. Recall that a central criticism of Gellner's theory was the problem of the intentions and agency of nationalist leaders, politicians, and others directly involved in managing the nationalist project.

Nationalist leaders are in many instances not fully aware of their role in connecting up the cultural entity of the nation with the requirements of industrialization, although the outcome is much the same as if they were. In the interplay of the subjective actor and objective social structure, the cultural dispositions of actors help to explain the social "feel for the game" of nationalism. In turn, social structures influence dispositions:

> Produced by experience of the game, and therefore of the objective structures within which it is played out, the "feel for the game" is what gives the game a subjective sense – a meaning and a *raison d'etre*, but also a direction, an orientation, an impending outcome, for those who take part and therefore acknowledge what is at stake ... And it also gives the game an objective sense, because the sense of the probable outcome that is given by practical mastery of the specific regularities that constitute the economy of a field is the basis of "sensible" practices, linked intelligibly to the conditions of their enactment, and also among themselves, and therefore immediately filled with sense and rationality for every individual who has the feel for the game (hence the effect of consensual validation which is the basis of collective belief in the game and its fetishes). (Bourdieu 1990, 66)

Bourdieu's interconnected concepts of *habitus* and *field* allow for power and culture to be considered at once in the form of social practices. Bourdieu's game analogy helps to describe habitus, which is "a realistic relation to what is possible, founded on and therefore limited by power" (1990, 65). Habitus is social structure observed within a field of social relations. It denotes the relations between cultural practices and the exercise of power. Cultural practices constitute the mode in which power is exercised. The "generative principle" of habitus provides a unity to social action, though it is not conscious. If it were, suggests Bourdieu, the practices would be, "stripped of everything that defines them distinctively as practices, that is, the uncertainty and 'fuzziness' resulting from the fact that they ... vary according to the logic of the situation" (ibid., 12). The *field* is the set of social relations under investigation, in this case Canadian regional and national spaces. The field is an arena of struggle in which actors seek to maximize economic, cultural, and social capital. The relationship between habitus and field is most important in understanding Bourdieu's model of social action, because habitus renders the field meaningful for actors, while the field conditions habitus via norms and rules, as shown in figure 3.1.

FIGURE 3.1 Bourdieu's model of social action

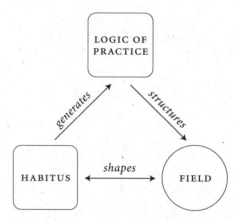

The distinctive cultural practices to be observed in the development of social identity in Canada are rooted in a discourse about the status of technology and are often, or even primarily, regional in character. A model of a nationalist logic of organizing in regions, to be presented in this chapter, has the potential to contribute to our knowledge of how nationalism continues to have significant effects. It can describe the relationship of localized cultural development with the "exostructure" of the nation-state – the administrative, military, and economic shell within which a national culture exists.

Identity and Unity in Canadian Regional and National Spaces

A number of scholars have called for sustained attention to the cultural means by which the logic of nationalism takes hold (Laitin 1998b; Mouzelis 1998; Beissinger 1998; Smith 2000). Wiley (2004) argues that a nationalist logic of organizing is at work in many places and times and appears in many forms, but that in an age of globalized communication the appearance and expression of nationalism must be observed with care: "The global spread of the nation as a social form through colonization and postcolonial nation-building did not assimilate all peoples and places into structurally equivalent national cultures. Even in spaces defined, formally, by nationalist logics, there are numerous aspects of social life for which nationality is largely irrelevant. In other words, we need not assume that we are always already 'in' nationally organized space, that the nationality of a particular social space is necessarily the most salient characteristic, or that nationally defined spaces today are national in the same way as they were in the past" (93).

In the Canadian context, a model of a nationalist logic of organizing in regions can show how national identity is developed and the extent to which it is distributed within the Canadian nation-state. The Canadian nation-state as we know it came into existence in 1867. As with all other nation-states, the affinity between nation and state in Canada is historically contingent. A model of a nationalist logic of organizing in regions suggests that cultural development takes place in a kind of pool of potential contributions to national culture. In this way, regional processes and practices shape nationalism.

The relationship of region to nation has often been noted by literary critics. Northrop Frye argues that social identity is primarily regional in nature and that it may in this way be distinguished from national unity: "The tension between this political sense of unity and the imaginative sense of locality is the essence of whatever the word 'Canadian' means. Once the tension is given up, and the two elements of unity and identity are confused or assimilated to each other, we get the two endemic diseases of Canadian life. Assimilating identity to unity produces the empty gestures of cultural nationalism; assimilating unity to identity produces the kind of provincial isolation which is now called separatism" (Frye 1971, iii). Frye's distinction highlights the use of literary texts in the constitutive creation of social identity. In a similar vein, Mary Louise Pratt observes that "peripheral spaces" are constituted in literary and other texts of the "central" space: "While the imperial metropolis tends to understand itself as determining the periphery (in the emanating glow of the civilizing mission or the cash flow of development, for example), it habitually blinds itself to the ways in which the periphery determines the metropolis – beginning, perhaps, with the latter's obsessive need to present and re-present its peripheries and its others continually to itself" (Pratt 1992, 6).

What is left out of the distinctions made by Frye and Pratt is the contemporary mediacized regional environment. Images of identity are now circulated "glocally." Symbols may be national in scope, but because of their continuous circulation by media they become part of the regional and local culture. The maple leaf of the national flag has always carried a somewhat esoteric and vaguely irrelevant presence in Western Canada. The flag has commanded respect, but because the maple tree is itself not indigenous to vast parts of the West it is something rarely seen in physical form. The maple leaf increasingly appears in a continually expanding mediascape of commercial applications. To provide just a few examples, we have the Roots line of clothing, the morphing logotyping on Air Canada jets, and previously, the logotypes of Canadian Airlines. The maple leaf is in the West a symbol of a symbol. Its constant circulation and exchange signifies in the region not the physical maple leaf but a cultural stylization expressed in both regional and national spaces. Many Westerners who have lived a long life in Canada have never seen a maple leaf. The maple leaf has become increasingly ethereal for the Western eye. At the same time, the symbol has become more regionally grounded. People come to regard the media incarnations of the maple leaf as part of the regional sense of place as its appearances increase in frequency in regional spaces. But the flow of symbols is not only from national space to regional. Local cultural concerns may be taken up as part of the discourse about national unity. The red serge was originally metonymic of the West but was later taken up as part of the national identity through the Mountie's capacity to symbolize order and good government, which was central to the social legitimization of national unity through the powers of a confederal state.

Technology and Nationalism as System and Process

In his propositions on the relationship of communications media to beliefs, values, and ideologies, Carey claims that "differentiated" national social systems differ significantly from "systematized" ones in terms of the role of communications media. The United States, he claimed, represented the latter form of social system, because individuals were "integrated laterally at many levels and built up geographically and functionally into a highly integrated social system" (1963, 168). In such a system, a crucial role of national media is that they create affinities between individuals and the national collectivity by "their weakening of intermediate structures which have their own media and communication systems" (169). In differentiated national social systems, on the other hand, by which we may say the regionalized Canadian political economy can be characterized, "minor media represent the interests of large but differentiated social groupings. Indeed they serve as a means of integrating the values and behavior of intermediate groups: labor, management, religious groupings, political interests, ideological interests. Such subsystems must not only define their own interests and thus produce communication systems, professional communicators, and media through which to define such interests and institutionalize values; they also must link at certain points in the integration of larger and larger units" (169).

The "social groupings" to which Carey refers include regions. In the same way that Gerald Friesen (2000) explores the meaning of Innis's claim that the native people had a fundamental influence on Canadian institutions, I want to explore Innis's gnomic claim that there have been regional "outbursts" of economic development in Canada and that regionalism is a key component of Canadian social development: "Regional parties have gained from the prestige which attaches to new developments. They have arisen in part to meet the demands of regional advertising, which in turn accentuates regionalism. They have also enjoyed the prestige which attaches to ideas imported from Great Britain, notably in the case of Social Credit and of socialism. The achievement of Canadian autonomy has, then, been accompanied by outbursts of regional activity" (1995, 272). This quotation is from an essay on economic staples, in which Innis assesses the comparative cultural development of the US, Canada, and Britain. The capacity of technology to shape social and economic institutions was one of Innis's most enduring intellectual legacies.

In some instances, a technology cannot easily be abstracted from a particular culture. The telegraph was managed as a state monopoly in European countries (Kieve 1973). The countries adopting the telegraph also embraced a standardized system of time, the notion of "instant communication," and the beginnings of remote medical diagnosis (Lubrano 1997). Lubrano describes some examples by which the literature and language of national cultures were deeply influenced by the telegraph. In the US, "telegraph tales involving heartfelt and sometimes unusual sentiments permeated the literature of the late 1800s" (124). In addition, new words were coined as the technology came into wider use. *Telegraph* itself replaced *telegraphic dispatch*. The principle and practice of standardization through Morse code was another consequence of the telegraph for language. After the adoption of the telegraph, the Roman alphabet became the standard set of graphemes used in international communication, displacing competitors such as Cyrillic script. Other, more nuanced aspects of standardization also took hold in cultures adopting the telegraph: "Short words gained an advantage over long words, words of precise meaning gained advantage over ambiguous ones, direct forms of expression gained an advantage over indirect ones, and local idioms became a disadvantage everywhere" (Lubrano 1997, 126). Cultural homogenization involves devising a practical means by which technology may be adopted and used within the society. National culture emerges from the local character of technology use as much as it does from language games.

The development of both regional and nationalist social identities relies on a reciprocal relationship between ideology and technology. Similarly, provincial separatism in Canada is indistinguishable conceptually from nationalist sentiments of alienation. The requirements for the emergence of provincial separatism are the same as those needed for nationalist secession. First, a prospective change must be coming into view on the economic landscape (Hiller 1987a). Without some potential improvement in the lot of most members of the population, there will be little likelihood that a secessionist project will attract the interest of individuals and groups living within the nation, province, state, or region. It should be noted that initiating or influencing such changes is generally beyond the capacity of individual actors, such as politicians, members of economic elites, and other prospective nationalists. They are broad historical shifts that create the social and political context within which the nationalist or regionalist actor works. The second requirement for separatism is not as far removed from the influence of individuals and groups. Before separatism builds at either the national or regional level, a disturbance must have occurred in the symbolic order. It is only through the familiar political relations and processes becoming unfamiliar that a large portion of the population is likely to consider a response as radical as separatism: "What do prairie and Maritime residents have in common in the era of the 1880s, post-Great War, and late 1970s? They are periods when the Canadian relationship to the international economy was undergoing significant change and, therefore, when the strain on particular sectors and communities within the country was greater" (Friesen 1994, 43–4).

Technology provides a focal point for social change in terms of shifts or disturbances in the symbolic order. The Missile Crisis described in chapter 2 constituted a disturbed symbolic order. The events described are still used by historians as a means of understanding the relationship of Canada to the US and, by extension, to the rest of the world. Technology provides an umbrella under which cultural accommodation takes place, and the modernist arguments put forward by Ramsay Cook underlined the potential for technology to symbolize progress and social development even, as in the case of missile production, the functional purposes and uses of the technology are only indirectly capable of contributing to society in these ways.

The symbolic order may be interpreted as one or more of the many aspects of the material or cultural economy. However, the importance of the disturbance in the development of a movement to secession as an option is clear. Babe synthesizes the main contention of C.B. Macpherson's work when he writes that, for Macpherson, "the major problems of our time are not primarily material but ideological, which is to say they are symbolic, and hence communicatory" (Babe 2000, 144). Symbols are exchanged in particular social contexts in which they are also shaped. Bourdieu argues that discourse as an object domain is the product of a complex set of social, historical, and political conditions. He observes the struggles of regional identity as being concerned with "the monopoly of the power to make people see and believe, to get them to know and recognize, to impose the legitimate definition of the divisions of the social world and, thereby, to *make and unmake groups*" (Bourdieu 1991, 221; author's italics). The case of regional identity formation in Canada elaborates on the use of symbols within a particular social context to develop an ideological framework within which communication is constituted in political and economic action.

Two periods of social transition or disturbance in the symbolic order of a region will be provided in subsequent chapters. First was the period from 1926 to 1943, from just before the beginning of the Depression until the prospect was emerging of reconstruction after World War II. In the case study from this period, the regional use of radio broadcasting for enabling democratic participation is described. Second was the period from 1947 to 1954, during which the discovery of oil set in motion new strategies of economic development in the province. A new state-sponsored oil company showed the local population that white-collar jobs would be one of the outcomes of a developing social identity.

A third period – 1970 to 1974 – is described in Adria (2000). During this time, massive oil revenues were pouring into provincial treasury and the question of how to deploy these revenues was becoming critical. An innovation normalizing the use of information technologies is put into place in the educational system as a marker of social difference. In each case, it is the local or regional culture that expends the social capital required to test the cultural development inherent in its regional project – the redesign of the communications infrastructure, changes in the capacities of citizens to participate in global economies, and the recasting of regional expenditures.

Defining Regions and Their Aspirations

A delimitation of the concept of the *region* is required, along with a comment about territoriality and nationalism. The concept of a region varies in discussions of culture and politics, even within North America. There are two common uses of the term. The first refers to the international aggregation of political interests. This usage is the more common one outside of the Canadian context. In his extended discussion on the terminology of nationalism, Connor (1994) states that regionalism properly refers to *trans*state identity, rather than *intra*state identity. He uses the term *sectionalism* in the same sense that regionalism is often discussed in Canada.

Likewise, Morley and Robins (1995) use *regionalism* to describe the emerging European supranational systems of media control, seeking to show the relationship of those systems to national identity. Similarly, Morris (1992) argues that national identity must be understood in relation to regional influences, but he is referring to international regions. In Canada, by contrast, *regionalism* is frequently used to refer to the political economy within a geographic area of the country. Regionalism is most commonly used in Canada to refer to *intra*national political consolidation of power. Watkins, for example, has used the term in this way: "The national history of Canada can be written around the theme of changing technologies, from the river economy of fur to the national economy of wheat to the regional economies of electricity. Except for short periods when fur and wheat were at their peaks, regionalism has been the rule rather than the exception of the Canadian experience, and Canadian nationalism has been largely a conscious strategy of pasting over the cracks" (1966, 294).

The pejorative cast to the use of the term *regionalism* that exists in other countries, particularly the US, does not necessarily exist in Canadian usage, as Gibbins notes: "Regionalism, although sometimes employed as a synonym for sectionalism, more commonly refers to amalgamations of states into geographical, cultural, economic or administrative regions, and to resemblances in politics and policies among such states. Regionalism is therefore viewed as a more integrative phenomenon than sectionalism…While in the United States sectionalism has become a value-charged term with few positive connotations, regionalism in Canada is both lauded and lamented" (1982, 4).

Canadian regionalism has come to mean the marshalling and aggregation of political influence from some geographical part of the country. Furthermore, *region* may be used interchangeably with *province* for the purpose of assessing economic and cultural development in Canada, since both regionalism and provincialism represent an alternative to national consensus and both arise from political claims grounded in territoriality (Friesen 1994, 1999). The use of the term *region* here in relation to a model of a nationalist logic of organizing in regions simply indicates that we are considering some socially cohesive subset of the national culture.

Finally, Hobsbawm (1990) uses the term *prototionationalism* to refer to a nationalist-like sentiment that was developed across national boundaries in the seventeenth and eighteenth centuries. He uses the example of certain Catholic sects that provided a protonational form of social identity that was to foreshadow and set the stage for the nineteenth-century European nationalist movements that occurred in Italy and Germany.

We should also note what is meant by nationalist aspirations, especially as they are expressed in regions. First, the nationalist logic of organizing in a region does not necessarily seek changes in territorial arrangements as a conventional nationalism would. Regional development may not be supported or influenced by the power of a local government. Whether there is a local government in direct proximity or not, cultural development in a regional sense must have a government with which it engages in a dialogue about relative autonomy. Indeed, the fate of the relative autonomy of the regional culture is what the regional project is all about. However, not all national states are complemented by provincial or state-level powers within their territories, although most will feature municipal or city administrations. A model of a nationalist logic of organizing in regions allows us to examine how local cultures will be accommodated, if at all, in the development of the national culture.

In Indonesia, for example, the Chinese nationals who had taken up permanent residence in the country since the late nineteenth century had a distinct influence on the development of Indonesian nationalism. The Indonesian Chinese had developed institutions that supported Chinese culture within the expatriate environment. The first and most influential institution was educational, the THHK (Tiong Hoa Hwe Koan – a society for the promotion of Confucianist thought and conduct): "The schools provided many symbols of the [pan-Chinese nationalist] movement, Kuo-yü [Mandarin dialect used in Indonesia by the Chinese], a knowledge of China's history, and a respect for Chinese cultural institutions were all encouraged" (Williams 1960, 198).

The other two institutions developed by the Chinese in Indonesia were related to business and to reading and writing: the Siang Wee (chambers of commerce) and the Soe Po Sia, which established a network of reading rooms and publishing enterprises throughout the country. So effective were the nationalist activities of the Chinese in Indonesia that members of the Indonesian political elite tried to learn from them as a means of improving their own nationalist organizing activities.

The lesson of the Chinese in Indonesia is that the logic of national organizing does not require a land base. A state or a territory is not always included in the nationalist logic of organizing. The pan-Chinese movement in Indonesia did not have territorial ambitions; neither did its members wish to return to China. Instead, the ancestral land served "as a spiritual home, but with the exception of some contract coolies and a few other migrants ... nobody seems to have given China much thought as a home to reside in physically" (Williams 1960, 200). Chennells makes a similar observation in relation to the goal of achieving a nation-state. There can be a varying balance between nation and state pursued in the activities of nationalist projects: "[N]ationalists do not seek only, or even necessarily, their own nation-state; in many cases, political objectives of securing cultural succour and official recognition are paramount" (2001, 4). It is in this sense that Chennells writes of a symbiosis that is required between nation and state in the nationalist project. A symbiotic relationship is characterized by mutually influential change. Action by one leads to a response by another, and the organic growth of the relationship is dependent on the actions of both. In Canada we may look to regions to observe important cultural accommodations by which the nationalist identity is maintained through the mutual development of technology and social identity. If the pursuit of territorial and state objectives has been overemphasized in studies of nationalism, technology has been overlooked as a key component of the nationalist logic of organizing. To support this claim, examples are provided from overlapping spaces in Canada in which nationalist organizing took place in connection to historical uses of technology.

Three Premises of the Model

The three premises for the argument to be presented for a model of a nationalist logic of organizing in regions are as follows: empirical links from regional cultures to the national culture, observable in *policy and decision-making*; the *relative autonomy of educational systems*, which implies that nation-states do not fully control educational regimes as

Gellner's theory requires; and the *logic of technology adoption*, which occurs in local and regional spaces and includes small-group interaction and the workings of the "demonstration effect." These premises provide a logical basis for the model, and the model is validated by the three cases, as shown in table 3.1. The premises are discussed in turn below, after which the model is proposed for a nationalist logic of organizing in regions.

TABLE 3.1 Premises in support of a model of the nationalist logic of organizing in regions

Premise in support of the model	Validating case	Implications for the modernist approach to nationalism
Empirical links in policy and decision-making	Radio (chapter 4)	Technological practices in regions influence those in national spaces
Relative autonomy of educational systems	Technology in educational systems (Adria 2000)	Educational systems are relatively autonomous within regions
Diffusion of innovations and the demonstration effect	Sociotechnology of a new organization (chapter 5)	The diffusion of innovations (such as nationism and technology) and the "demonstration effect occur in regional spaces

EMPIRICAL LINKS IN POLICY AND DECISION-MAKING

"National communication systems function," Carey writes, "to highlight socially significant or threatening deviance from the basis of national consensus" (1963, 210). The first premise for the development of a model of the nationalist logic of organizing in regions is that there are empirical links that can be established in policy between the experimental or developmental uses of technology that take place in *regional* contexts and the *national* symbolic and practical applications of the same technology. Innovations – social or technological – may be traced in longitudinal studies from their origins or early uses in a regional culture to their appearance and development in a national culture.

Policymaking may therefore be "adjudicated" within a region before it is adopted within the national culture.

Such a policy link between regional and national spaces will be examined in chapter 4. The historical case of radio in Canada reveals the connection between regional uses of a communications technology in the 1920s and 1930s and that same technology's ultimate contribution to national social identity as reflected in national broadcasting policy in the 1970s. Radio broadcasting in Alberta during the 1920s and 1930s functioned as a coordinating technology for deliberative democracy. This innovation was taken up nationally but only until it became the subject of a change in the national broadcasting policy. The ultimate cultural trajectory of radio in Canada saw the positioning of radio's content, along with that of television, as a subject of state regulation for the purpose of maintaining cultural sovereignty.

RELATIVE AUTONOMY OF EDUCATIONAL SYSTEMS

Basic education is at the heart of Gellner's concept of the nation-state, and this is the departing point for the second premise. Gellner states that "centralized exo-education ... complements ... localized ac-culturation" (1983, 34). The kind of centralized educational systems associated with modern industrialized countries is required in Gellner's modernist theory of nationalism because "sub-units of society are no longer capable of self-reproduction" (Gellner 1983). A universal, standardized program of basic education within the nation is a critical feature of the system by which the occupational mobility required by industrialization is achieved.

Yet educational systems have historically been recognized and accommodated within *regional* – not national – regimes of control. Within those regimes, educational systems remain relatively autonomous. While educational systems are contested by many and varied social groups, local and regional government's control of schooling is an almost universal principle in the modern nation-state. Efforts at nationalist control of education are unlikely to take hold. The relative autonomy of educational systems in connection with the rise of national educational systems has been considered in historical accounts of the character of national cultures. Ringer (1992) examines the political and economic contexts for the emergence of educational ideals in

Germany and France in the late nineteenth century, a time of public debate in those countries about the fate of the classical education in response to emerging technical and vocational educational programs. He argues that educational systems had a role in social reproduction through their inculcation of specific cultural values related to social status. Ringer shows that within a historical phase of transition, when new occupational groups are moving toward higher social status, educational systems provide a kind of buffer for these changes, by which older occupational groups maintain their high social status for a period of time, until the educational system becomes only marginally influential in the political economy.

In Germany and France, the national culture had a formative influence on the respective theories of education, along with associated practices, but in markedly different ways. The national culture characterized the development not only of the educational systems in the two countries but social identities and political and economic fates as well. Ringer observes comparatively that a "mandarin culture" emerged in Germany during this period. This culture consisted of professors, civil servants, lawyers, doctors, secondary teachers, and Protestant pastors. The mandarinate functioned as a status elite rather than as an economic class. As a status elite, the group did not exercise direct control over the development of the German economy. Instead, it exercised influence and maintained its high social position through its development of a culture by which economic class stratification was maintained. A central theme in the cultural work of the mandarinate was *Bildung*, or "cultivation," through education. The ultimate goal of the educational system in Germany was for the student to experience fully the aesthetic and moral ideals expressed in society's canons. French positivism, on the other hand, presented the educational goal of interaction with a text, which was a very different experience. Students in France were to immerse themselves in the ideas of the "great minds" that produced them. Ringer writes that, "[a]t some level ... French reformist social science bracketed the hermeneutic distance between particular readers and particular texts" (Ringer 1992, 315). In the German educational system, the student's interaction and communion with "great minds" were mediated by literary and scientific texts, while in France the text was to be read largely in isolation from the biography of the author. The reasons for this difference had to do with the historical and cultural roots of the educational systems. The French academics, when compared with their German counterparts, were more likely to refer to the political dimension of their proposed changes: "They wrote as if more fully aware than their German counterparts that they were participating in a political confrontation, which was a species of class conflict as well. This was probably true in part because they had experienced the direct impact of changing parliamentary majorities upon educational policy. The political system in which they participated trained them, as well as their audiences, to see educational alternatives as political ones; they were almost forced to state their positions accordingly" (ibid., 159–60). The national culture that Ringer describes instilled a disposition *toward* certain possible alternatives for reforming educational systems and *away* from others. Some policy options therefore came to appear more attractive than others. Ringer argues that educational systems reflect changes in social class much more quickly than they do changes in social status. As a result, they continue to reproduce the structures of social status even after these structures have become disassociated from those of social class. Educational systems must be regarded with an eye to the "presence of the past." Historical notions of social status may persist within educational systems, allowing for them to "act back" upon the social hierarchy.

Education and schooling within the national culture represent a relatively autonomous social system. Changes in the educational system occur in relation to changes in social class and social status at varying rates. If there are variations in such dimensions of the national culture as these, the social structure of the educational system may be expected to vary *within the national culture.* This suggests that educational systems, contrary to Gellner, are relatively autonomous and may therefore feature significant regional differences. The argument in relation to the model of a logic of national organizing in regions is that studies of nationalism must take into account regional cultural activity of this kind, because it has the potential to shape a national culture in decisive ways (see, for example, the case study in Adria, 2000).

DIFFUSION OF INNOVATIONS AND THE DEMONSTRATION EFFECT

The third premise for a model of nationalist logic of organizing in regions is to be found within the population theory of the adoption of technology (Rogers 1995). The nationalist state finds legitimacy in part by the demonstration effect, that is, by showing how the economic and political program will function in practice. Of the many potential nationalisms in the world, only a relatively few have or will become active nationalist projects. As noted in chapter 1, a nation may usefully be defined as a group of people sharing a culture and recognizing one another as fellow nationals. There are many such nations, but few large enough and finding themselves in a social context in which their claims to a nation-state would have any chance of success. Of those nationalist projects that survive, only a fraction will become successful in aligning themselves with a state. There are many more potential than actual nationalist movements In fact, there are thousands of languages in the world, yet fewer than two hundred nation-states: "Most of the potential nations, the latent differentiable communities which could claim to be nations by criteria analogous to those which somewhere else have succeeded, fail altogether even to raise their claim, let alone press it effectively and make it good" (Gellner 1983, 49).

Within those nationalist projects that are successful in their objective of creating their own state, a population of regional projects is continually roiling. This "pool" contains potential adopters of technology, and the adoption of technology among individuals and groups, including groups within a national polity. We may ask why one nationalist movement rather than another emerges from such a pool. The answer in part is that the demonstration effect helps to consolidate social identity.

The term *demonstration effect* in studies of nationalism refers to a social event such as a *coup d'état*, or popular overthrow of a government (Gellner 1983; Amir 2004), which is given attention by outsiders. It may be defined as a revolutionary event in one location that stimulates or influences a revolutionary event elsewhere. Although the term is often used to refer to *social* events, its theoretical roots lie in the theory of the diffusion of innovations, which is concerned with how and at what rate *technological* adoption occurs within a population. The theory of the diffusion of innovations has developed increasingly complex models of the adaptation of technologies and other innovations, including social innovations. Diffusion of innovation is defined as the process by which (a) an innovation (2) is communicated through certain channels (3) over time (4) among members of a social structure

(Rogers 1995). The basic principle of the theory is that the messages of communications media alone cannot account for the adoption of a technological or social innovation. Instead, potential adopters seek interpersonal sources, such as friends and family members, as sources of expertise and experience. Diffusion of innovations therefore posits a two-step flow of, first, message receipt through a media channel, and, second, validation of the message through interpersonal communication. Adoption models give attention to the decision-making process by individuals, the social networks within which these individuals are embedded, the flow of information in the social networks, and the process by which the technology adoption occurs.

In his study of nationalism in the Brabant revolution of the eighteenth century, van den Bossche points to the two-step flow of diffusion of innovations theory in his consideration of cultural evidence for the strategies of elites at the early stages of a nationalist project: "[W]hen confronted with change, individuals are motivated by their desire to understand what they perceive as an increasingly unfamiliar and perturbed world. When this leads to communication at mass level, we may assume first that the sense of upheaval affects a large proportion of the population; and second, that the social representations thus communicated have at least the potential of providing reassurance and meaning for that large proportion of the population" (2003, 503).

The use of metaphors and visual communication techniques such as political cartoons can help to show (a) whether elites were creating a participatory space in which dialogue about the nationalist project could take place and (b) whether the form of the dialogue was one that could be taken up in conversation by smaller groups of people. Following the two-step flow of diffusion of innovations theory, the demonstration effect suggests that technology "teaches" by becoming an exemplar of the benefits of nationalism. By creating "news" about the innovations inherent in a nationalist project, the demonstration effect stimulates face-to-face conversations about the project. The demonstration effect is mediated through technology and its subject is technology. The demonstration effect may in some instances be rooted in a distant part of the world. A consequence of such an event is that a nationalist movement is provided with a view of what is possible in its own part of the world. Alternatively, the demonstration effect may be found in the homeland of the nationalist project. The demonstration effect is important for sustaining a nationalist ideology, because it provides the continuing and unifying rhetorical thread for the many individuals and groups involved in the nationalist project (Gellner 1965). Chapter 5 provides the example of a new organization whose mandate and mission were connected to state economic priorities and whose symbolic function constituted the demonstration effect within the region.

A Model of a Nationalist Logic of Organizing in Regions

Theories of nationalism turn on two epistemological dimensions. The first of these is the status of national culture. Theories of nationalism differ fundamentally on the question of whether a national culture is invented, as we said in chapter 1. The primordialist/perennialist view is that cultures exist at all times but they appear to historical observers only at certain times, particularly during periods in which the symbolic order is disturbed. The modernist view is that culture is aligned with the requirements of the material economy. Industrialization follows the route of least resistance, and that has most often been the route of the development of a consistent culture. Modernizing societies draw upon the cultural resources that they can find; if need be, they imagine a national culture into existence. Technology has a role in identifying and disseminating texts in support of an invented tradition and an imagined community.

The second epistemological dimension involves the relationship of social actors to power. The primordialist/perennialist view is that a national culture is an enduring phenomenon and that it would exist in one form or another, even without a state home. Social actors, including nationalist leaders, draw on the cultural resources of the nation in order to fulfill national aspirations. The modern view is that national cultures exist in response to the political work of social actors, who are fatefully influenced by the political economy. For Hobsbawm (1990) and van den Berghe (1981), the fictive aspect of culture is complete. Culture is fully at the disposal of manipulative elites. For Gellner, a more nuanced interplay exists within national projects, combining authentically felt cultural identity and the deployment of that culture for political purposes. Table 3.2 depicts the key theories of nationalism in relation to one another. The distinction between primordial/perennial approaches to nationalism is arrayed along the dimensions of culture in the left-hand column, and power in the top row.

TABLE 3.2 Propositions of key theories of nationalism, highlighting the nationalist logic of organizing in regions (adapted from O'Leary 1998, 77)

Nations are	primarily tools of manipulative elites or ideological masks for interests	primarily expressions of authentically felt identities	*both* tools of elites and authentic expressions of identities
perennial and permanent features of humankind	Van den Berghe (1981)	Herder (1969) and most nationalists	Fichte (1931)
(often) continuous with premodern *ethnies*		Armstrong (1982)	Hutchinson (2005)
		Anthony Smith (2000)	
(mostly) modern	Brass (1991) Hobsbawm (1990)	**Nationalist logic of organizing in regions**	
			Gellner (1983) B. Anderson (1996) Connor (1994)

Gellner's modernist definition of nationalism was as follows: *Nationalism is primarily a political principle, which holds that the political and the national unit should be congruent.* A definition of nationalism that takes up the operational requirements of nationalism as Gellner identified them would incorporate both the logic of organizing that informs nationalist projects and the role of technology in constituting the communicative practices of nationalism. The actions of individuals and groups within regions are bound to be counterposed at one time or another to the interests of the nationalist project. While nationalism's final outcome is a homogenous culture at the heart of a new political accommodation or acquiescence within the administrative home of the state, preliminary stages involve conflict and resistance. My definition of nationalism is therefore as follows: *Nationalism is a logic of political organizing that seeks the symbiosis of nation and state in local, regional, and national spaces through the mediating and demonstrational uses of technology.* Examples will be provided to test this elaboration of the modernist definition of nationalism. In particular, each of chapters 4 and 5 provides an extended case study validating this definition and the model to be presented.

The processes and practices of a nationalist logic of organizing in regions engage Gellner's factors contributing to the principle of "one state, one culture." The movement toward such an alignment requires movement along certain planes, which include, as noted earlier, literacy, education, and communications media, as well as innovation and occupational mobility. The institutions of literacy, education, and communications media are commonly supported by the national state, which allocates funds to ensure reliable communication systems, beginning with postal and telephone systems, which are supported, in turn, by a high level of literacy through the basic schooling system (Osborne and Pike 2004). Through the processes and practices of nationalist logic of organizing in regions, widely held interpretations of messages are created within the national culture. For example, the transition from oral to literate communication, a requirement for the development of nationalism in Gellner's theory, takes place largely through the processes and practices of a nationalist logic of organizing in regions, many of which are counterposed to modernism and modern nationalism. Regional processes and practices may significantly influence the range, scope, and form of these planes of social transformation, when translated into opportunities and benefits for individuals. These factors are shown in relationship to regional contexts of social action in figure 3.2 and discussed in the subsequent section.

FIGURE 3.2 Model of nationalist logic of organizing in regions

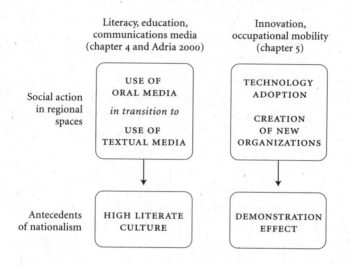

Literacy, education,
communications media
(chapter 4 and Adria 2000)

Innovation,
occupational mobility
(chapter 5)

Social action
in regional
spaces

USE OF
ORAL MEDIA

in transition to

USE OF
TEXTUAL MEDIA

TECHNOLOGY
ADOPTION

CREATION
OF NEW
ORGANIZATIONS

Antecedents
of nationalism

HIGH LITERATE
CULTURE

DEMONSTRATION
EFFECT

LITERACY, EDUCATION, AND COMMUNICATIONS MEDIA: COMMUNICATING ABOUT IDENTITY

The first component of figure 3.2 to be discussed is literacy, education, and communications media. These are the capacities by which a national culture becomes aligned with a national state. The literate, educated citizen who consumes media is oriented to certain messages rather than others. Beyond their rather broad consciousness of themselves as individuals, people are oriented as well to their status as citizens of the nation. This is the meaning of the "banal nationalism" that Billig (1995) describes. Literacy, education, and communications media are interrelated capacities because each is successively dependent on the other. The literate citizen is one who can consume the products of communications media. Although moving images and photographs are integral to the success of media content, there is always a reliance on text to provide the specific meaning of images. The internet as an advertising medium, for example, requires consumers to type on a keyboard and to use basic skills of literacy. In turn, communications media affirm the social and economic benefits of an educated population. Similarly, educational systems produce literate citizens, and the political legitimacy of these systems is based on the sentiments of a literate population, regardless of their political allegiance (Bendix 1977). Liberal, conservatives, and populists alike support the social value of education, though for different reasons. The significance of the interdependence of literacy, education, and communications media for the nationalist project is that in their mutual social affirmation, these capacities serve to support the creation of a high literate culture. The abstraction and individuality inherent in reading and writing are central to such a culture's epistemological foundation in the written word. In her analysis of the rise of a literate public, Eisenstein notes that a high literate culture is one opposed in some respects to that of a local community: "The displacement of pulpit by press is significant not only in connection with secularization but also because it points to an explanation for the weakening of local community ties. To hear an address delivered, people have to come together; to read a printed report encourages individuals to come apart" (2003, 103). The relationship of oral and textual media is thus of particular importance to the development of a national culture.

ORAL AND TEXTUAL MEDIA: TRANSITIONS IN AND THROUGH TECHNOLOGY

Technology, including communications media, is an antecedent of nationalist projects, as shown in figure 3.2. Scholars have continued to bring social and historical perspectives to the varying influence of particular media on the development of nationalist projects. Mexican radio throughout the middle of the twentieth century, for example, has been examined to reveal the effects of its modern form and its antimodern orientation (Hayes 2000). Radio is characterized by the intense modern characteristic of "flow." Radio programming is continuous and irreversible, suggesting something of the rapidly changing nature of modern life. It is also a medium by which antimodern oral communication predominates. Ancient techniques such as mnemonics (using acronyms as memory aids, for example) and formulaic phrases are combined with modern techniques for maximizing the economic returns for owners of the broadcasting enterprise.

As the sociologist Alvin Gouldner (1976) has pointed out, the alternating historical process of first generating ideas, and then deploying technology in support of those ideas, requires the continuous production and circulation of symbols using communications technologies. Ideologies give life to large-scale social movements such as nationalist projects. This is possible only through the use of the technology of communications media. For many nationalist projects, the newspaper has been the medium by which nationalist ideas have gained wide circulation.

The use of communications media is associated with a nationalist logic organizing in regions because of its bias of either oral or literate culture. Each communication medium has a bias by which the message of its use, regardless of the content of the message, is established: "The most important and persistent message is generated by the medium itself, by the role which such media have acquired in modern life. That core message is that the language and style of the transmissions is important, that only he who can understand them, or can acquire such comprehension, is included in a moral and economic community, and that he who does not and cannot is excluded. All this is crystal clear, and follows from the pervasiveness and crucial role of mass communication in this kind of society. What is actually *said* matters little" (Gellner 1983, 127). Gellner was clearly influenced by medium theory, as developed by Innis and McLuhan. His description of media's structuring influence echoes that of medium theory in its attention to the structuring influence of technology. Medium theory suggests that the material means by which culture is developed has a significant influence on the development of that culture. For Heyer (1988), "[h]ow we organize and transmit our perceptions and knowledge about the world strongly affects the nature of those perceptions and the way we come to know the world" (xiv). Deibert develops a variation on medium theory that he calls "ecological holism" – an "open-ended, nonreductionist, thoroughly historicist view of human existence that emphasizes contingency over continuity, both in terms of the trajectory of social evolution and the nature and character of human beings" (1997, 17–18). A medium favouring oral communication (the radio, audio playback devices, the telephone, public address systems, and the like), encourages the transition from an oral to a literate culture. Such media are in some instances transitional to nationalism, because of the tension between their modern and antimodern characteristics. While reflecting the progressive technological identity of other media, they are based in the ancient techniques of verbal and nonverbal symbols and of the modulation of the human voice. Textual media are implied by a medium such as radio, in that the writer-speaker is the central figure. Texts are therefore a ground for the figure of radio. The transition from a predominantly rural society to a mainly urban society involves the development of a high literate culture in which a much larger audience is engaged. A medium that favours literate culture, such as a book or a literary journal, encourages the further development of nationalist logic of organizing in regions and, in turn, nationalism:

> Socially, the typographic extension of man brought in nationalism, industrialism, mass markets, and universal literacy and education. For print presented an image of repeatable precision that inspired totally new forms of extending social energies. Print released great psychic and social energies in the Renaissance, as today in Japan or Russia, by breaking the individual out of the traditional group while providing a model of how to add individual to individual in massive agglomeration of power. The same spirit of private enterprise that emboldened authors and artist to cultivate self-expression led other men to create giant corporations, both military and commercial. Perhaps the most significant of the gifts of typography to man is that of detachment and noninvolvement – the power to act without reacting. (McLuhan 1964, 157)

Media favouring both oral and literate culture, such as the internet, encourage the maintenance of a literate culture, because they create a mediating space between the oral and the literate even as they create new texts. The internet allows for the flourishing of both oral culture and high literate culture while providing for the transition from the former to the latter. The nationalist logic of organizing in regions "cools out" the local expression of oral culture – it gives expression to it, while creating a new space for the development of a high literate culture.

HIGH LITERATE CULTURE: CHANNEL OF THE NATION-STATE
A homogenous culture is the medium of the nation-state, the channel by which national communication takes place. As shown in figure 3.2,

this is a key antecedent of nationalism. The national culture is based on a universally literate citizenship. Local acculturation is coordinated and developed through national institutions. Individuals and groups negotiate the circumstances of knowledge construction in connection to many institutions, but the school, university, college, and vocational institutes are at the centre of such negotiations because of their power to confer the legitimacy of knowledge through the state's licencing power to award degrees and certificates (Foucault 1995; Gellner 1983; Ringer 1992). A literate culture is required for the standardization of variants of speech and writing, which in turn lays the foundation for a mobile population that makes, in Gellner's words, "every man a clerk."

A nationalist project entails the adoption of a high literate culture as the common cultural resource for the nation. A high culture is rooted in texts and the printed word. Practices relying on the oral transmission of ideas give way to practices rooted in a relatively narrow textual idiom – or oral practices that can easily be translated into text. In rural and remote communities, media technologies allow for this transition from small-scale communication accomplished through oral practices to communication that may be transmitted to and understood by the national community. When introduced in rural communities in North America in the 1920s and 1930s the family radio, for example, became a symbol of progressivism. The cultural uplift provided by radio – symphony concerts, lectures, and so on – was a highlight of early radio broadcasts. The radio for the farm family was a modern device by which the larger world could be introduced into the home. Its rhetorical mode, however, was not modern, as noted earlier, but antimodern, relying on the ancient tradition of the writer-speaker. The voice on the radio used the rhetorical techniques of mnemonics, formulaic phrases, and other means by which memory, the glory of the storyteller, could be maintained. In the early days of radio broadcasting, the listener in the rural community was oriented to both the modern and antimodern faces of radio and was therefore positioned to make a transition to literate culture.

The language of a high literate culture is ideological, because ideology is "that part of consciousness which is focused linguistically on public projects" (Gouldner 1976, 81). The interlinked strands of literacy, ideas, and nationalism are indivisible. An "ordinary language" adopted through universal literacy is at the heart of a national culture. Using such language, it is possible, as Gouldner points out,

> to have rational political discussion with others who commonly possess the shared language it provides. Somewhat more precisely: ideology is grounded in the utilization of an ordinary language, but it is the restructuring of an ordinary language in special ways: partly by selectively focusing the ordinary language on certain public projects; partly by changing certain of the meanings of the ordinary language, giving it a somewhat new or extraordinary meaning, extended redefinition, or focusing; partly by taking certain parts of ordinary language and making them newly problematical, thus assigning a new significant to them; partly, by the invention of new signs ... Ideology, then, separates its adherents from nonbelievers, allowing the former to cooperate with one another for the achievement of their special projects, while at the same time allowing discourse with nonbelievers; allowing continued efforts to win them over to the ideology. Ideology is both a bridge and a moat; it both separates believers from nonbelievers and, also, connects them. (1976, 81)

The national culture is one of transitions and cultural accommodations, both within and without. It is accommodational, negotiated, and contingent. It little resembles the *a priori* cultural package presented by nationalist leaders. A model of a nationalist logic of organizing in regions provides a window on the accommodations, negotiations, and contingencies of local and regional settings.

INNOVATION AND OCCUPATIONAL MOBILITY: BUILDING THE ECONOMY OF THE NATION-STATE

Industrialization requires a society in which innovation is valued for its capacity to encourage economic growth. Innovation may be social, economic, or technological. Technological innovation is given primacy in nationalist rhetoric, because it is deployed for the constant enlargement of production. It is by technological innovation and the expanding economic product that a nation is admitted to the world of nations. In such a society there are limited cultural restraints on the movement of individuals to higher levels of socioeconomic achievement. Beyond their symbolic value as remnants of idealist heritage, religion and tradition must not have a particularly influential place in allocating individuals to occupational or social positions. Literacy, education, and communications media are interdependent social capacities by which a high literate culture is established. They give primacy to *process over product*. Innovation and occupational mobility may be considered complementarily as a kind of spectacle leading to the demonstration effect, an illustration of what the nationalist project is all about – and therefore emphasizing *product over process*.

TECHNOLOGY ADOPTION AND NEW ORGANIZATIONS: PUBLICLY VISIBLE PROMISES OF NATIONALISM

Gerald Friesen writes that the method of communication used in a historical era "shapes popular assumptions about how the world works" (2000, 5). While Friesen limits himself to orality, print, and text as the technologies by which people communicate, we may also add the socioetechnologies of communications, including education and bureaucratic organizations. Innovations in such sociotechnologies provide a medium of communication as rich as a language. Indeed, the organization can be viewed as being constituted by the written and spoken word (Taylor and Van Every 2000). Signficantly, in Friesen's evocative analysis of "plain Canadians," much attention is given to the socially formative influence of such varying organizations as the Hamilton steel works, Imperial Oil, and socialist political movements. Organizations are established with economic and political purposes, but they are cultural constructions. Within organizations, we can observe the means by which social relationships are established, cultural meanings established, and historical narratives taken account of. They are communication media by which social identity is developed. Other theorists have adopted the category of technology in a way that both considers the effects of technologies as corollary to the effects of communications media and also consider organizations and other sociotechnologies as part of the category of technology. In Deibert's "ecological holism," for example, organizations and institutions are a category that blends into the category of technologies as the zone between society's "web of beliefs" and the "geophysical environment"

(1997, 38). Organizations, as much as technologies such as communications media, are useful as tools; they are also culturally embedded and constitutive of society.

The fruits of innovation and occupational mobility include the establishment of organizations that reflect the priorities of the nationalist state. Technology adoption is important for its symbolic meanings and its concrete benefits. The nationalist logic in regions develops themes of the national identity through the localized understanding of technological adoption and practice. The idea of social cohesion within a region is associated with the material means by which it functions in a mutual relationship of legitimation (Gouldner 1976). Individuals and groups come to understand the social meaning of a technology by its deployment and use at the local and regional level. Even the very *national* instance of the armed forces, which exist for the protection of national interests, have regional implications for social identity. A new program of submarine manufacture will have its first and most lasting influence on social identity in the region in which blue-collar, clerical, and management staff work and live.

THE DEMONSTRATION EFFECT: NATIONALISM AS SPECTACLE

The final part of figure 3.2 to be considered is the demonstration effect. The uses of technology in relationship to nationalism may be regarded as belonging to either or both of two primary categories: mediating and demonstrational. The *mediating* use of a technology involves publicly justifying state action within the national community, while transmitting messages in support of the nationalist project. In many countries, including the UK, Australia, Canada, and Sweden, a national broadcasting agency, supported by public funding, has been established for that purpose. The legislation establishing such agencies requires that the national character be reflected in and promoted by the national broadcaster. In broadcasting enterprises of all kinds, technology is a carrier of cultural information in the form of television shows, radio broadcasts, and so on. It is also a structuring influence in regional, national, and international economies, because it can help create and change patterns of trade and development. Culture and power therefore exist historically in a mutual relationship of development. Mediating uses of technology are associated with literacy, education, and communications media, as noted earlier.

The *demonstrational* use of technology involves obtaining, developing, or using technology in support of a nationalist cause. An example would be military technology, such as aircraft, tanks, and firearms, which may be used to enforce either a national unification or separation. The technology used by armed forces has always been central to the maintenance and extension of nationalist programs. Commonly used definitions of the state highlight the importance of technology in relation to nationalism. These definitions distinguish the state from other organizations or entities by pointing to the state's monopoly on the use of violence that is approved by law. The state deploys the technology of warfare outside its borders and of criminal justice within.

The use of technology may be *both* demonstrational and mediating. Radio has been used as a mediating technology in the development of national identities in many regions of the world. Radio has supported nationalist projects by promoting cultural and political events in which the glory of the national culture is celebrated. It has helped to revive folk musical traditions and lore, as well as local dialects and linguistic variants. It has also been used to demonstrate the socially progressive character of a national identity. By providing universal access to radio signals as a public benefit available to members of the nation, the national identity is enhanced and made more attractive to the population. By embracing communications technologies, the character of the national identity is promoted as aspiring to modernity and to the promise of economic and social advances. Radio's social uses in such instances would therefore be both demonstrational and mediating in support of nationalism.

The demonstration effect is both symbolic and concrete, and it can be observed in such developments as new organizations and technology adoption. A nationalist logic of organizing in regions provides a population of social outcomes from which a nationalist movement may select. Such a pool consists of projects and engagements from which the nationalist program may draw in order to demonstrate its viability. Gellner argues that a much smaller number of nationalisms take hold than could potentially do so. In the same way, a new organization may show the benefits of industrialization in a region – and thereby the accrued advantages of nationalist associations with the organization. Or it may not. What is suggested here is that a stock of potential instances of the demonstration effect must be available in order for nationalism to cohere, and the regional and the local provide the most fertile ground for their continuous seeding.

Potential Insights of a Model of Nationalist Logic of Organizing in Regions

The insights to be gained by applying the model that has been outlined in this chapter concern knowledge about the prospects for particular national projects. Examining historical cases in which technologies have been used in the development of social identity can reveal the practices of nationalist organizing and the ways that such a nationalist logic combines with other logics, such as those of commerce, corporations, and bureaucracies.

Applying our knowledge of a nationalist logic of organizing in regions, we might gain a better understanding of the sequence of events within which nationalist projects unfold. There is value in knowing why a nationalist movement develops at one time in history, rather than at some earlier or later point. If it is clear that elites promulgate the nationalist principle in significant part to secure their own future status within the society, it is less clear why they do not begin preaching the gospel of nationalism sooner rather than later. The question of sequentiality, in turn, has implications for how studies of nationalism are carried out. Van den Bossche (2003) calls for studies that evaluate the processes by which the "anchoring" and "objectification" of nationalist ideas take place in a given society. These processes correspond to the stages of development in which the new ideas of the nationalist project find a welcome place among previous ideas, and in which the new ideas become familiar over time. The local and the regional provide a context in which new ideas about nationalism can be examined at close hand.

Another potential insight of the model concerns the role and influence of technology. The model allows us to ask how and to what effect technologies – including communications media and sociotechnologies – are used by nationalist programs. Nationalism is a modern phenomenon that involves mass audiences mediated by communications media. The technology associated with the development of nationalism may be examined in order to identify the kinds of messages that are favoured at particular stages and the nature of the influence of the technology on the national consciousness. It is in the local and regional context that the uses of a new technology can be examined in relation to the development of the "new" ideas of nationalism as they are circulated in local, regional, and national spaces.

Between the micro-interactions of daily conversations and exchanges and the convergence of narratives and myth in the creation of a national culture is a mid-range of practices that become familiar to the vast majority of a population. This process has gone largely unexamined in the literature of regionalism and nationalism in Canada. A model of a nationalist logic of organizing in regions provides a lens through which may be viewed this middle range of social practices by which nationalism develops. Each of the next two chapters discusses a case of technological development and the relationship of this technology's adoption and use to regional and national identity.

4

THE TRIBAL DRUM OF
NEW MEDIA

[W]hen the CBC is instructed by Parliament to
do what it can to promote Canadian unity and
identity, it is not always realized that unity and
identity are quite different things to be promoting, and that in Canada they are perhaps more
different than they are anywhere else. Identity is
local and regional, rooted in the imagination
and in works of culture; unity is national in reference, international in perspective, and rooted
in a political feeling.

Frye 1971, ii

Nationalist projects have a split character. They are modern in their
forward orientation. They prescribe modern solutions for traditional
problems. They also refer to the wisdom of a long-expired *volk*. They
cultivate – and have the capability to revive – dying or dead traditional
idioms. The modern side of the Janus face of nationalism appears as
technology, but technology itself reflects both the modern and antimodern character of nationalism. Radio, for example, while carrying
the message of both modernism in its technological form, is a medium
through which forgotten language practices and in many instances
forgotten languages, may be given new life.

Regionalism is a primary means by which the logic of nationalist organizing is distributed within the space of the nation. The examination of historical cases in which technologies were used in the development of social identity can reveal the practices of such a logic and the ways that it combines with commercial, corporate, and bureaucratic logics. It can also reveal the sequence of events by which nationalist projects develop and suggest something of the strategies that have been successful in such a project.

The problem of how to avoid the circular logic of the construction of identity within an already existing entity continues as a thread in theoretical debates. Hall (1998) suggests that we are considering two somewhat incommensurable dimensions of identity, which are discourses into which individuals are "interpellated" on the one hand and the subjectivities that allow individuals to express their status as subjects within these same discourses: "It has never been enough – in Marx, in Althusser, in Foucault – to elaborate a theory of how individuals are summoned into place in the discursive structures. It has always, also, required an account of how subjects are constituted" (Hall 1998, 13). We can say that the Canadian nation-state existed before the period described in this chapter, in that nationalism, the joining of nation and state, occurred formally in 1867 with Confederation. We are therefore considering a pre-existing entity. But even in the two decades following 1867, the completion of the Canadian Pacific Railway was informed by a rhetoric of nationalism (Charland 1986). The Canadian nation-state continues to change, and this change either supports or detracts from the affinity between nation and state. Nationalism waxes and wanes. The Canadian nation-state's stage of change in relation to the broadcasting technology of radio was, in the 1920s and 1930s, crucial. Broadcasting was thereafter to follow one social trajectory in Canada and not another. In twentieth-century Canada, new technologies were reshaping social identities in a way that encouraged the continuing development of a national identity.

Literacy, education, and communications media are interrelated social capacities required for the development of nationalism, and the practices and processes by which this is accomplished occur in regional spaces as well as national spaces. The cultural truism that "our culture is different than others" links the modes of literacy, education, and communications media. Their shared idiom, or pattern of difference, becomes associated with the distinctiveness of the national culture.

Radio reaches back to oral traditions that for some communities are sensed to be under threat. It can encourage the transition to a literate culture by providing a basis for social unity in the present while pointing to a technologically modern future. The historical case of radio described in this chapter illustrates the process by which changes in social identity occur. Incremental departures occur from what is known and familiar in cultural life, while some measure of continuity is maintained with the familiar. This principle supports the theoretical approach taken by van den Bossche in describing the symbol representation and meaning-making by which a nationalist project is formulated: "Social psychology... identifies the two mechanisms through which social representations perform the construction of meaning and identity. A first mechanism strives to anchor strange ideas, to set them in a familiar context. This implies the transferral of those ideas to our particular sphere where we are able to compare and interpret them. The purpose of the second mechanism is to objectify these strange ideas, in the sense of rendering something abstract into something almost concrete" (2003, 503).

The oral medium of radio allowed for the accommodation of cultural and economic difference through an appeal to the democratic potential of the technology. The novelty of radio at the time was contrasted with the print conventions that were criticized as being associated with a central government. The radio voice provided a sense of what unified the region, in this case a political opposition to the federal government. The case reveals as well the link between regional uses of a communications technology and the resulting contribution to national social identity. Radio broadcasting in the 1920s and 1930s functioned as a coordinating technology for deliberative democracy. The logic of nationalist organizing in the case involved two practices: contesting the social meaning of a new technology through the presentation of a preferred meaning, and linking that preferred meaning to the political cohesion of the region, which was positioned as being in opposition to the national political arrangement. The nationalist logic of organizing in a region that may be observed was therefore opposed to bureaucratic and corporate logics of organizing.

In this chapter, the case of radio broadcasting is examined in the context of its simultaneously modern and antimodern influence on social identity. The link from the regional to the national level of identity will be traced in the chapter through an examination of national broadcasting policy in Canada. The case reveals the connection between the regional uses of a communications medium in the 1920s and 1930s and that same technology's ultimate contribution to national social identity as reflected in Canadian national broadcasting policy in the 1970s and thereafter. The nationalist mandate for radio broadcasting was established in 1932 with the creation of the Canadian Radio Broadcasting Commission (later called the CBC), but the implications and stakes for local and regional interests are revealed in this case to have extended into the 1950s with the abandonment of a particular model of radio use developed within a region. The cultural trajectory that radio adopted in Canada resulted in the content of both radio and television becoming the subject of state regulation for the purpose of maintaining the nation-state's cultural sovereignty, which Raboy (1990) describes as representing "missed opportunities." The regional use of radio described in this chapter is one such missed opportunity.

Social Identity and the Uses of Technology

From 1926 to 1952, the role of democratic participation through radio broadcasting was a residual issue not yet resolved in Canada. Social identity in Alberta in the early- to mid-twentieth century was developed in part by taking up the *national* issue of the social uses of radio broadcasting. Both William Aberhart and E.A. Corbett contributed to the development of national identity in Canada by demonstrating a potential social trajectory for radio as a coordinating technology for deliberative democracy. By demonstrating a potential social role for radio broadcasting, this regional experience contributed to the development of national identity. That role was ultimately rejected through a succession of federal policy decisions culminating in the regulations on broadcasting content that were instituted two decades later. The cultural trajectory of radio that actually occurred in Canada subsequently was the positioning of radio's content, along with that of television, as a subject of state regulation for the purpose of maintaining cultural sovereignty. In examining the role of radio in contributing to both regional and national identity, we may examine the regional resources of social action and cultural identity upon which a nationalist project draws.

Both Aberhart and Corbett were concerned with what radio – and, by extension, the modern mediated social world – was to introduce to the social and political culture of mid-century Canada. Aberhart broadcast his sermons and political lectures through his Calgary Prophetic Bible Institute, and these continued after his election as premier. Corbett was involved in the establishment of an early educational broadcasting station, CKUA Radio in Alberta, and, through his later work with the Canadian Association for Adult Education, the *Canadian Farm Radio Forum* and *Citizens' Forum*, both of which were broadcast nationally on CBC radio. The radio programming of Aberhart and Corbett became a notable thread in the social, cultural, and political life of Alberta. Both cases represent experiments in deliberative democracy that, although highly popular, were left aside for another model of media use in Canada.

These examples have been considered previously, albeit separately, as illustrations of the interplay of politics, media, and public education in Western Canada (Irving 1959; Schultz 1964; Faris 1975; Laycock 1990). The social genesis and cultural meanings of the two broadcasting projects are compared here in order to examine the role of technology in the development of social identity in a region and, in turn, in the resolution of residual problems of nationalist projects. It is argued that there are regional backcurrents within nationalist configurations of communications technologies and social identity. Radio in Alberta provides a rich example of how such cultural developments emerge. In turn, the development of a national social identity in Canada has drawn on the economic, cultural, and political activities occurring in provinces and other regional spaces.

Radio Broadcasting and Alberta's Political Culture before World War II

National identity and nationalist projects are, like much of modern social life, mediated by communications media. Technologies, and particularly communications technologies, have an intervening and influential role in the development of national identity and establishment and maintenance of modern nationalism and the nation-state (Gouldner 1976; B. Anderson 1996). Radio has figured in the development of national identities in many countries (Mrázek 2002; Hayes 2000). Radio has characteristics and uses that are both modern and antimodern. This tension is parallel to the oppositional character of nationalist projects. Radio may at once mediate an image of the nation as technologically advanced, leaving tradition behind in its forward movement, while at the same time evoking tradition and the preindustrial mode of interpersonal communication, especially in its capacity to enliven fading or forgotten linguistic practices and even dialects and languages (Fishman 1996). Nationalist projects, too, make their case to a prospective national community based on the projected forward destiny of the nation, while paradoxically appealing to a cultural birthright that is claimed to reach back to premodern times. Through radio, ancient texts give voice to the dead, to "those who will no longer speak" and in whose "single dead body" the nation identifies itself (Taminiaux 1996, 95). The preindustrial ideals of nationalism include order and stability, with a hierarchical system of governance, as well as heterosexual passion and reproduction, which symbolizes wholesome, virile males and chaste, beautiful females. By drawing on such preindustrial ideals, nationalist movements established a metaphorical pool of images from the past, while pointing to a portrait of a transcendent future: "[N]ationalist discourse was forced to bridge the divide between tradition and progress, past and future. Although the nation assumed a distinctly antimodern politics and aesthetics, it was still fundamentally tied to the modern forces of capitalist production, colonial expansion, and bureaucratic organization under which it developed and spread. In particular, the modern form of the nation has been described as a 'mass-mediated' form, reliant on modern technologies of mass communication for its particular structure and content" (Hayes 2000, 16-17).

Radio programming is characterized by the intense modern mode of flow. It is continuous and irreversible. Hayes (2000) refers to the effect of this feature as a "fleeting presence," which "mimics the modern experience of reality as ephemeral and forward moving" (20). Radio's modern emphasis on strength and movement has been masculine in gender and evocative of a national consciousness. Douglas (2003) points out that it was men and boys who "brought this device into the home, and tinkering with it allowed them to assert new forms of masculine mastery while entering a realm of invisibility where certain pressures about manhood could be avoided" (215).

Today, radio broadcasts incorporate ancient techniques for rendering the flow of sounds meaningful. Techniques such as mnemonics and formulaic phrases are still used in radio broadcasting, combined with techniques for maximizing the economic returns for owners of the broadcasting facilities: "Broadcasters actively work to re-create the sociability and interaction of oral settings by developing intimate, chatty forms of radio talk and using live audiences for radio performances. In this way, radio's sound format gives listeners a sense of continuity with older forms of verbal intimacy and community" (Hayes 2000, 22).

In the 1920s and 1930s, the political culture in Alberta since the establishment of the province in 1905 had been developing under two political parties, the United Farmers of Alberta (UFA) and the Liberals. Public discussion of political issues was still being carried out mainly in face-to-face discussions, underpinned by the newspaper, which itself was not yet widely available in rural areas. The newspaper had not yet accomplished in Alberta what it done elsewhere in Canada – particularly in Québec, Ontario, and the Atlantic provinces – which was to promote a common, politically and socially unifying vernacular idiom. These years coincide with the beginning of Alberta's move from the farm to the city. The new medium of radio was deployed in a hinterland region in which the rural population was economically desperate and the urban population was beginning its growth, which by the early 1950s would reverse the poles of political dominance. The rural society of pre-World War II was to become a predominantly urban society by mid-century. The relative shift in the population had not been completed, however.

Along with an uneasy relationship of rural-dweller to city-dweller was a nascent distrust of the political power of Central Canada. Radio had not found a place in the social and political life of Canada. The question of who would have the ultimate voice in how radio would be used and for what social purpose was, in fact, very much in play: "Canadians had just begun to ask basic questions concerning the ownership, control, and use of radio by the end of the 1920s. By the time voluntary association leaders had become aware of the educational potential of the medium, a variety of interests were vying for its ownership and control" (Faris 1975, 61). On the other hand, radio's modern character arose out of its capacity to create new and larger cultural communities than had been previously possible. In radio converged the simultaneity of interaction, which had been heralded fifty years earlier by the telegraph, and the homogeneity and mass audience developed earlier by the newspaper. The disjuncture of radio from these older media lay in radio's capacity to form a mass audience participating simultaneously in an event. The simultaneity of radio occurred in the modes of speed and flow, in contrast with the traditional mode of incremental, organic growth. Radio thus represented a break with previous modes of time and space. Douglas (2003) states that, in the US, "people perceived the rapidity with which radio listening redefined everyday life as unprecedented ... This perception that Americans were feverishly overthrowing the past – its pace and substance – was embodied in the radio boom" (218).

The combined modern and antimodern characteristics of radio reveal its capacity as a mediating technology within the expansion of national projects. Radio transmits messages about social identity – hence its "mediating" role – but it also has a "demonstrational" capacity. The adoption and use of radio publicly reveals the socially progressive character of a nascent national identity. By providing universal access to radio signals as a public benefit available to members of the nation, the national character is enhanced and made more attractive to a wider population. By embracing communications technologies, the character of the national identity is developed symbolically and materially as a modern project.

The modern medium of radio in the Alberta of the 1920s and 1930s resonated with a growing urban population in the province. Radio represented the modern qualities of flow and speed in a region of Canada in which modernity had much to offer in terms of a promised higher standard of living. At the same time, the antimodern, oral facet of radio appealed to inhabitants of the sparsely populated rural areas of the province and had the potential to give voice to simmering economic and political discontent. The large and simultaneously participating audience that radio made possible was to coalesce in two broadcasting initiatives that were to have enduring implications for the social and political culture and identity of Alberta and, indeed, of Canada.

Radio and Deliberative Democracy

William Aberhart and E.A. Corbett introduced the social innovation of deliberative democracy to Canada with their radio broadcasts, beginning in the 1920s and 1930s. Deliberative democracy is an approach to political participation that has theoretical and historical roots in the ancient Greek *agora*. Processes and practices of deliberative democracy seek an alternative to the instrumental rationality characteristic of modern political systems. Instrumental rationality represents the capacity of the state to "devise, select, and effect good means to clarified ends" (Dryzek 1990, 14). Approaches to deliberative democracy may involve modification, supplementation, or repudiation of instrumental rationality. They posit an ideal form of public dialogue that is an alternative to the logic of instrumental rationality: "Communicative rationality is rooted in the interaction of social life. Communicative *action* is oriented toward intersubjective understanding, the coordination of actions through discussion, and the socialization of members of the community. Communicative *rationality* is the extent to which this action is characterized by the reflective understanding of competent actors ... [C]ommunication is concerned in part with the coordination of action, so communicative rationality cannot totally replace instrumental rationality; rather it can only restrict the latter to a subordinate domain" (Dryzek 1990, 14).

Deliberative democracy may be distinguished from the simple feedback mechanisms of media programming. Phone-in radio shows, television talk shows, and web polls seek a response from a mass audience, but they are developed as products for sale. They are less than fully deliberative, because they are formalized and emphasize etiquette and avoid substantive conflict (Habermas 1989). Deliberative democratic processes are not necessarily dialogical, in the manner that conventional notions of participatory democracy suggest. This is the departing point for many critics of Habermas, who acknowledge and accept that while we have lost the face-to-face agora of debate by co-present individuals and groups, we have not necessarily lost publicness as a quality of discourse. Thompson, for example, seeks to reinterpret deliberative democracy in the context of new communications technologies: "By 'deliberative democracy' I mean a conception of democracy which treats all individuals as autonomous agents capable of forming reasoned judgements through the assimilation of information and different points of view, and which institutionalizes a variety of mechanisms to incorporate individual judgements into collective decision-making processes. The deliberative conception of democracy focuses attention on the processes by which judgements are formed and decisions are taken ... [T]he legitimacy of a decision stems from the fact that the decision is the outcome of a process of generalized deliberation" (Thompson 1995, 255).

With the advent of radio in the 1920s and 1930s in Alberta, Aberhart and Corbett each operationalized through experiments in radio – and much before the full implications of a mediacized public sphere had taken hold – their well-developed ideas about how and why public dialogue and political discourse could be combined, with radio functioning as a coordinating technology. Aberhart developed the idea of radio programming for a public audience, but through private production. Radio would be used for what may be called individual "accreditation," based on the idea that radio programming should coordinate and correct the doctrine held by members of a group. A significant goal of this programming would be political mobilization. The audience would listen motivated by a desire to be part of an informed group. For his part, Corbett developed the idea of radio programming that would be public in both production methods and audience. Corbett's "radio as adult education" was based on the belief that radio programming was a public good and could best be deployed for the purpose of the betterment of both individual and society.

William Aberhart, Democratic Participation, and the Accrediting Function of Radio

In 1925, William Aberhart established the Prophetic Bible Conference in Calgary, soon to be renamed the Prophetic Bible Institute. His experiments with radio began in 1926, and starting in 1932 his talks on economics were broadcast regularly over CFCN, a private Calgary station.

About 300,000 listeners in Alberta and parts of Saskatchewan and the northern US tuned in to the Institute's religious services broadcast each Sunday. These broadcasts brought together through the airwaves people who were disillusioned during a period of economic hard times by an increasingly cosmopolitan tone in their local church and community experiences. With the rise of the two major urban areas of Calgary and Edmonton, churches had begun to be concerned with social problems to the relative exclusion of more spiritual matters (Schultz 1964). Aberhart preached about the literal meaning of scriptures in a style that was direct, configured around actual events in the world, and implying a personal call to action. A typical program combined a personal anecdote with some popular wisdom. An excerpt from one of the early broadcasts in 1927 conveys to the audience the wisdom inherent in the family, which is to be found in simple principles arising from practical work: "My father used to drill me on this. He often said, 'My lad, do not pay too much attention to every squeal you hear.' 'Remember always,' he added, 'that it is the lean bacon that squeals the most.' The mockers we have always with us, they say" (Aberhart 2005).

In 1936, after he had been elected premier, the opposition demanded an end to the radio broadcasts that had brought Aberhart into the public forum. Aberhart responded by suggesting that there was moral decay and hypocrisy behind the demands. In 1936, he was using a series of rhetorical questions to buttress his argument:

We acknowledge that there has been some objection taken to our broadcast. It has been resolved that we should be put off the air on Sunday afternoons, because it is claimed that we are mixing religion and politics and that is interfering with the happiness of some. Are any of the words of Christ such as not to be fit to be discussed on Sunday? That would be a strange attitude to take. I'm satisfied that the majority of the people of this province are not so religiously sanctimonious as to believe that all reference to politics on Sunday is sacrilege. That would even outstrip and go beyond the strictest of the puritanists. Since when have these diehard politicians become so ultrareligious? [Applause.] Surely politics should not be so corrupt and vile as to have all reference to it on Sunday tabooed. (Aberhart 2005)

Aberhart's broadcasts were characterized by the voice and mode of morality, which in rhetorical terms is the "righteous master analogue" (Bormann 1980). The rhetorical and the moral were consistently combined in the broadcasts. The fundamental criticism of political and social elites in Aberhart's messages was that institutions and processes were corrupt. The techniques of rhetoric and oratory were used to establish and develop the righteous analogue, as Innis notes in his comments on the characteristics of regional development: "As a teacher Aberhart had acquired an extensive vocabulary. Graduates from his school were scattered throughout the province and his influence persisted as a factor facilitating effective appeal. His Bible Institute and appeals to the Bible and to religion were used with great effect. Bible texts and hymns and semi-biblical language were designed to attack usury, interest, and debts. The conversations and parables of the founder of Christianity were repeated with great skill, notably in attacks on the money changers" (1995, 274).

Innis also mentions Aberhart's "attacks on older types of communication such as the chain newspapers dominated by eastern control" (ibid., 274). In 1937, the premier attempted to have the Social Credit League, an organization with close ties to the party, purchase the newspaper the *Calgary Albertan*, along with a radio station that the paper owned, an attempt that ultimately fell through (Bell 1993, 111). The "difference" of radio as a new medium was discursively associated with the "difference" of Alberta's economic development and Social Credit's express antipathy to Central Canadian interests. The distinctive and innovative characteristics of radio were connected in this way with the new and particular problems of a province in a new era. One of the actions by the Social Credit Government that attracted international attention was the legislation to allow for censorship, the Accurate News and Information Bill of 1937. The legislation was never given assent by the lieutenant-governor. This bill was intended to muzzle the newspapers in the province for their criticism of government decisions. Radio was not seen by Aberhart to be in need of such censorship, perhaps because it was already being controlled by the federal government.

The radio broadcasts that accompanied and gave impetus to Aberhart's political career were part of a deliberative mode of communication that was consistently enacted throughout the 1920s and 1930s.

By the winter of 1933–34, study groups for the discussion of Social Credit doctrine were established throughout the province. In the city of Calgary alone, there were sixty-three groups functioning during spring and summer 1935 (Irving 1959, 63). The meetings took place in community halls and in private homes from Monday to Thursday. On Fridays, at the Institute itself, there were meetings attended by more than two thousand people. The radio programs were complementary to the large auditorium meetings of the institute and the "Cottage and Parlour Meetings," which were held in people's homes. The home meetings were to be organized using guidelines and protocols written by Aberhart himself and distributed through the mail. Social Credit represented a rethinking of the democratic relationship between elector and elected and of the political relationship between region and federation. Individuals were encouraged to discuss this new conception of the polity for themselves. The attractiveness of the political ideas presented was enhanced by the participative and engaging nature of the informal discussion groups that were formed across the province.

The masterly interactive techniques used by Aberhart were reflected in a key event in 1935, which set the stage for Aberhart's direct entrance into provincial politics. With the Depression, Aberhart had been drawn to the Social Credit doctrine of Major Douglas. At the same time, the UFA Party began to weaken with the provincial election of 1930. Aberhart began his dissemination of Social Credit theory from outside of the formal political system, intending to influence the UFA Government's policies but decided eventually that a new political party was supported by many. Radio provided immediate feedback to that effect early in 1935. Aberhart was considering the question of whether he would continue to use his considerable political influence in the province to influence the United Farmers of Alberta Government to take up the principles of Major Douglas's Social Credit or whether – as he actually decided to do – he would found a new political party to allow for more direct political action. On a spring evening during one of his radio broadcasts, he took a "straw poll," asking for listeners to let him know whether he should start his own party. The response was clear. Some 93 percent of respondents of an estimated 200,000 listeners felt a new party should be founded with Aberhart as leader (Schultz 1964, 197).

At the time of the straw poll, Aberhart had already been conversing with his audiences for more than a decade. The blend of the righteous master analogue, religious doctrine, the didactic voice, and a call for personal action had been developing for some time. Radio listeners heard direct responses from the institute audience in Calgary during the broadcasts. They could then respond by mail to the invitations by Aberhart to write to ask him questions and to receive, in turn, written information about the ideas being discussed on radio. Study groups were established, in which individuals discussed, in the early years, the religious doctrines, and in the later years, the political principles of Social Credit. At institute meetings, a response was not only assumed by Aberhart or measured indirectly by audience survey, it was invited and then broadcast to the larger audience on radio, as illustrated from this excerpt from 1927: "I want to ask you a question to just assist me in the prayer. Will all those who now acknowledge God as the giver of all good gifts and who will love and worship him no matter what comes, will you say out loudly, 'I will'? [Audience responds: 'I will.'] Thank you. Any others who didn't say it before, will you say it now, 'I will'? No others? I ask you once more. You didn't all say it. Who else will say I acknowledge God as the giver of every good gift and I shall love and adore him no matter what happens. Will you say, 'I will'? A few more said, 'I will.' Any others who'd like to say, 'I will.' Now will all those who said 'I will' lift your hands to heaven like this? Thank you very much. Put them down. Let us bow our heads in prayer" (Aberhart 2005). This direct response was to be extended through the establishment of the study groups. Radio was used selectively and strategically, providing a plenary session by which other rhetorical activities were to be coordinated: "Audiences throughout the province were held together by correspondence. Large numbers wrote in and subscribed small amounts. Their names were read over the radio and comments were made on their letters" (Irving 1959, 274).

Radio was thus used in two ways by Aberhart. First, it was used to coordinate a comprehensive set of rhetorical activities, including fundraising, ideological training, study groups, and the maintenance of a sympathetic social network. The system of deliberation depended not only on radio but also on a reliable postal system, which required roads and railways, along with a relatively high level of literacy, undergirded by a system of basic schooling (Osborne and Pike 2004). Without this comprehensive system of communication, the straw polls and discussion groups could not have functioned as effectively as they did. Second, radio itself was contrasted discursively with other media such as the newspaper, which were portrayed as being under the control of an antipathetic federal government. Radio was portrayed as new and unadulterated.

The personal nature of the broadcasts was not unique in the 1920s. The period in which William Aberhart used radio for political purposes was exemplified by the messages of President Roosevelt, who had broadcast twenty-eight of his "fireside chats" during his three terms in the 1930s and 1940s. Radio was also used during Roosevelt's presidency for public, non-political purposes. The US Office of Education produced eleven educational network programs. In addition, there was the Federal Theatre Program, as well as the broadcasts provided to local stations by the Departments of Agriculture and Interior (Sterling and Kittross 2003, 225). What set Aberhart's program's apart was the deliberate, organized, and effective program of broadcast and reception, discussion in small groups, and feedback from the groups, which then was fed forward to influence the content of the subsequent broadcast.

E.A. Corbett and Radio for Democratic Participation

Edward Annand Corbett began working in the Department of Extension at the University of Alberta in 1920. During that time, Extension was involved in travelling libraries throughout the province, as well as a library whose fifteen thousand volumes were circulated by mail to remote communities, a "package library system" for use in debating and discussion clubs, lantern slides for use by schools and churches, and correspondence courses in economics. In the early 1920s, the University of Alberta began broadcasting lectures on CJCA, a radio station operated by the *Edmonton Journal.* Then on October 11, 1926, Extension established its own radio station, CKUA, which carried talks, music, and lectures and information for farm audiences. The station carried live orchestral music, along with recorded music and live drama. Farm information was broadcast regularly on the station. During the first decade of CKUA's operation, Corbett was active as the western representative for the Canadian Radio League, which lobbied for public ownership of radio broadcasting facilities, in support of the Aird Commission recommendations of 1929, which called for public control of radio broadcasting. As a university teacher he also worked with members of the cultural elite in Canada, such as John Grierson, director of the National Film Board, in putting his ideas into the public realm as educational and cultural development projects (Reichwein 2005). Corbett was a pioneer of the adult education movement in Canada, but his initial experiences were fatefully shaped by rural Alberta. Adult education for Corbett was less "cultural uplift" than a meeting of personal circumstances and the capacities of the local university: "The old concept of university Extension as a series of lectures on such remote subjects as the foreign policy of Patagonia or Tennyson's Use of the Comma would be wildly out of place in a pioneer community whose people are, of necessity, interested in such mundane questions as fertilizers, soil surveys, how to winter fall pigs, how to organize and manage a co-operative or credit union, how to build a root cellar, fix a tractor, or build a community hall" (Corbett 1957, 63). Ironically, it was because of his knowledge of Aberhart's broadcasts that Corbett was at first hesitant to become involved in using radio for the purpose of broadcasting public education programs. In his work with the University of Alberta, Corbett would travel around the province introducing lectures on English literature or simply showing slides or films to audiences in the evening. Aberhart's own radio broadcasts competed with Corbett's presentations for the attention of rural populations that Corbett visited. Attendance at Corbett's lectures usually suffered in deference to Aberhart's (Corbett 1957, 106).

Corbett became the founding director of the Canadian Association for Adult Education (CAAE) in 1936. It was in this national capacity that Corbett expanded the application of his ideas, first sown in Alberta, of the use of radio produced through public agencies and consumed by a broadly based audience. By autumn 1939, the first of the *Canadian Farm Radio Forum* and *Citizens' Forum* programs were broadcast across Canada on the national radio network of the CBC. Organized by the CAAE under Corbett's leadership, these programs supplemented and extended the activities of adult-education agencies and institutions in Canada, such as the universities, provincial departments of education and agriculture, and voluntary organizations across the country.

The two broadcast series, for which Corbett became well known in Canada, were always associated with a plan for small-group discussion, the establishment of such groups in communities, and the production and distribution of print materials to support the groups' activities. The approach was strikingly similar to that of Aberhart, although Peers (1969) believes Corbett was influenced not by Aberhart but by the British Broadcasting Corporation's experiments using discussion groups. Comments from the discussion groups that Corbett established were generated and cycled back for incorporation into subsequent programming. The *Canadian Farm Radio Forum*'s slogan was "Read-Listen-Discuss-Act," and there were well-organized methods to ensure that this series of activities was actually possible for listeners. For example, a series of sixteen pamphlets, entitled *Canadian Farm Problems,* was produced by Québec's Macdonald College. These pamphlets were, in Corbett's words, "admirably suited for study group purposes," and there were groups organized to allow individuals to ask questions about the current broadcast (Corbett 1957, 146).

The size of the audiences for the CKUA, *Canadian Farm Radio Forum,* and *Citizens' Forum* programs may be measured in the millions of listeners. The *Citizens' Forum* broadcasts alone attracted some half a million listeners in the 1940s and 1950s. The audience for any particular *Canadian Farm Radio Forum* program was 1 percent or less of the farming population, but the steady interest in the programming suggests that there was strong interest in maintaining the benefits of organized discussion of ideas about social problems and potential solutions. The number of people participating in discussion groups may be measured in the thousands. The *Citizens' Forum* registered more than 1,200 groups in 1943–44, declining to about three hundred groups per year until 1952 when the program ended.

The *Canadian Farm Radio Forum* maintained more discussion groups over time and reported more successful citizen action reports than did the *Citizens' Forum.* Registered discussion groups in the *Canadian Farm Radio Forum* numbered one thousand in 1943-44 and rose in 1949–50 to a level of 1,600 groups representing 21,000 participants.

The program's topics from 1941 to 1953 included "the problems of distribution as opposed to the often more technical questions of production which departments of agriculture and agricultural colleges were equipped to answer" (Faris 1975, 99). The most frequent topics were as follows:

- the legislated and systematic marketing of farm products
- international problems of marketing
- rural education
- community life and action
- prices and price spreads
- cooperatives and credit unions
- health services.

The discussion groups can reasonably claim to have had an influence on at least one significant issue of public policy in Canada. According to Faris, "the discussion of health services was the most concentrated [in comparison with cooperatives and credit unions], being mostly presented in 1943–45 when the CFA [Canadian Federation of Agriculture] and other movements actively promoted a national health plan" (1975, 99).

Regional Contestation of the Uses of a New Technology and the Social Fate of Radio

The programming regimes of both Aberhart and Corbett were the subject of intense political criticism. This is the first glimpse of the link between regional and national identities. Aberhart and Corbett had contributed to the development of national culture in Canada by addressing a contradiction in Canadian cultural life and broadcasting policy, one that had not yet been resolved, which was whether radio would be used for the purpose of cultivating democratic participation in Canada. The alternating expression of new ideas about a social and economic project on the one hand and the deployment of technology in pursuit of that project can be seen in the two cases. This dialectic occurs at the regional level as much as it does at the national level.

The problematics of ideology occur and are often resolved by those living at the social and political margins (Innis 1951). The region remains a space in which experimentation may take place – and is in fact expected to take place (Friesen 1994). The fundamental unresolved political issue in the 1920s and 1930s in Canada had to do with the role of the state in providing relief from the Depression; subsequently, another issue was the role of the state in reconstruction efforts following the Second World War.

The question of the ownership of radio broadcasting facilities was still being debated in the 1930s and 1940s in Canada. During this time, private broadcasters knew that, with a decision of the British Judicial Committee of the Privy Council in 1932, Parliament had confirmed its exclusive jurisdiction over radio broadcasting in Canada. Many radio-station owners expected that their operations would be expropriated, although some members of the Canadian Association of Broadcasters were "quite sympathetic to nationalization" (Vipond 1992, 240). The ownership question was closely related to the cultural question of how radio would be used, since the design and interpretation of messages in media is based on whose interests are at stake in terms of both broadcaster and audience. The fate of radio's use in association with techniques of deliberative democracy may be considered by reference to the series of policymaking decisions made by the federal government following the work of Aberhart and Corbett. This policymaking adjudicated – indirectly and perhaps unconsciously – on the possibility of communications technologies having a significant role in broadly based deliberative democracy in Canada.

The *Citizens' Forum* in the early 1940s was hosted by two Canadians who would eventually make their mark on Canadian cultural life. Novelist Morley Callaghan was the on-air host, and philosopher George Grant was involved in the program as secretary of the CAAE, working with Corbett. A conference preceded the establishment of the broadcasts, in which consultation with institutions and agencies involved in adult education took place. In 1943, the *Citizens' Forum* intended to invite CCF representatives M.J. Coldwell and David Lewis, in addition to Prime Minister Mackenzie King, to a series to begin in autumn. A program entitled, "Of Things to Come – A *Citizens' Forum*." was to be a radio series devoted to a consideration of postwar reconstruction. As the plan for the program took shape, it became clear that criticism of the sitting government was likely. Parliamentary assistant Brooke Claxton wrote to the prime minister that the series should all but be cancelled: "The programme must be fundamentally changed ... [Left-wing labour lawyer J.L.] Cohen must not be allowed to speak. If anyone moves now it will be said to be in consequence of government preju-dice. Probably the best thing to do is withdraw all invitations and start over. [CBC producer Neil] Morrison and [Host and novelist Morley] Callaghan should be fired as incompetent" (memorandum to Prime Minister King, 1943).

Claxton was a linking figure between the Aberhart-Corbett era of broadcasting and the one that exists to this day. Claxton was responsible for drafting and carrying forward the strong criticism of the *Citizens' Forum*. He was then to become the founding chairman of the Canada Council in 1957, following the recommendation of the Massey Com-mission. The Canada Council would provide funding for the creation of Canadian culture. This was a new approach to the role of commu-nications technologies in Canadian cultural and social life, in which the federal government would regulate a space for cultural production by Canadians, as a response to the increasing influence of US culture in Canada.

In the several years following 1945, cultural development was being explicitly discussed in Canada, as it was in Europe and the US. Two royal commissions had addressed the emerging role of broadcasting in the development of national identity. The Aird Commission of 1929 on broadcasting (the "Aird Commission") and the Massey-Lévesque Commission of 1949–51 on national development and the arts (the "Massey Commission") were to have significant effects on public policy. The Aird Commission recommended public ownership of radio broad-casting. As a historical public event, the commission also signalled the beginning of a pattern of engaging in public consultation on broadcast policy development (Gasher 1998). The Massey Commission argued that it was the task of the country's artists and intellectuals to dedicate themselves to the development of a distinctly Canadian culture and identity. Each would support the other. The federal government's duty would be to support artistic production. The national character was to be reflected in and promoted by the CBC. The Massey Commission's comments and recommendations in regard to radio in particular were that artists and musicians should receive funding for their work, that commercialism from the private broadcasters was encroaching on the programming decisions of the CBC, and that lectures and talks should be given more emphasis in proportion to musical production:

> For six days a week, from midnight throughout the morning and until seven o'clock in the evening, it broadcasts news, sports commentaries and music, broken only by a daily ten minute talk of interest to women and by a fifteen minute news commentary. The music broadcast throughout the day is almost entirely recorded popular music. These stations live by advertising; and spot announcements crowd their programmes sometimes to the limit tolerated by the regulations. An analysis of the programmes of another important private station in a large centre revealed that spot announcements in the permitted hours occurred at an average frequency of five each hour ... After a careful consideration of the evidence available, we are convinced that only very rarely can limited revenue be advanced as an extenuating circumstance for this inexpensive and unimaginative programming. (Massey Commission, 39–40)

The Massey Commission responded to concerns about US influence on Canadian cultural development by "proposing to defend the nation's future with the safeguards of high culture" (Berland 2000, 16). Vincent Massey himself had, as early as 1928, written to O.D. Skelton, undersecretary of state for External Affairs, of the need for a publicly owned broadcasting system (Vipond 1992, 209). The commission's envisioned response to external threats to Canada's sovereignty was to be the creation of a high culture of modernism, in which technology had a role to play in the symbolic and concrete creation of a productive and growing economy and society. Subsidies for the production of Canadian content would be provided as a kind of cultural antidote to the influx of US broadcasting content. Information, education, and entertainment were to be the functions of radio broadcasting, under the auspices of the CBC, which held national responsibility for regulating all broadcasting in the country. Against the recommendations of the Massey Commission, this powerful role was to be undercut in 1957–58 with the creation, on the recommendation of the Fowler Commission on Broadcasting, of the Board of Broadcast Governors (BBG), which took away regulatory powers from the CBC. The BBG became the Canadian Radio and Television Commission Broadcasting (CRTC) in 1968.

The *Canadian Farm Radio Forum* was commended in special terms by the Massey Commission; in 1957, the program was examined favourably by UNESCO. As a result of this examination, similar programs were set up in India, Ghana, and France. Still, the program was to come to an end within a couple of years. Both Aberhart and Corbett had pioneered the use of radio as something other than simply a channel for information and cultural content. It invited dialogue. It differed from the educational programming that would be developed in the 1960s and 1970s by provincial broadcasting agencies such as TVOntario, in that it did not anticipate the outcomes of that dialogue.

It is possible to follow the fate of the two programming regimes to federal cultural and broadcasting policy that occurred in the 1950s and 1960s. Subsidies and maintaining a broadcasting space within which Canadian content (CanCon) could develop became the theme of significant government action with regard to communications technologies and culture thereafter. In 1960, the BBG put in place CanCon requirements for television. By 1970, the BBG's successor, the CRTC, had decided that at least 35 percent of popular music broadcast by commercial radio stations each week must be Canadian selections. Pierre Juneau was the chair of the Canadian Radio and Television Commission during the 1970s and became the public face of the CanCon regulations during that period. Juneau's (1985) comments some years later about Canadian culture, after he had become president of the CBC, have been echoed in many ways in the discussions and debates thereafter about the role of Canadian media in relation to culture; the theme is that the dominant concern for the state is that Canadian programming content must have a significant presence in Canadian media:

A country that has nothing to say to the world is a dull country; no story to tell, no songs to sing, no picture of itself, no stimulating ideas. (2)

Broadcasting ... is the most powerful manifestation or mirror of our culture. (3)

[A] great step would be made if we arrived at a national consensus that culture is not a luxury. (18)

The democratic meaning of media was also of concern to Juneau. He wrote that in "bringing culture to every Canadian ... broadcasting makes culture democratic" (16). But Juneau did not see democratic function as an appropriate core concern of broadcasters. Instead, regulation and an accommodation within the economic market were necessary. He suggested, in fact, that government regulation was not enough, that there needed to be a built-in market incentive for broadcasters to develop and broadcast CanCon: "Canadian content quotas aren't enough; these people are businessmen and have a right to be, and we must devise the means to make the production of Canadian productions profitable to them" (16).

By 1970, radio was following the prescription of the Massey Commission, which was that the state's primary concern must be to ensure that Canadian culture must find its rightful place in the world. CanCon rules were and are based on regulation of the content of radio, not on public ownership or involvement through ongoing deliberative activities. They rely on a regulatory, but not economically active, state. The logic of the Canadian approach to radio is based on diversity of programming, on the notion of wider audience choice. A nationalist mandate for broadcasting was established in 1932 with the creation of the Canadian Radio Broadcasting Commission (to become the CBC), but the case examined in this chapter reveals the stakes for local and regional communities. Albeit briefly, Aberhart and Corbett provided a significant alternative to the nationalist mandate.

The Fate of Media Use for Deliberative Democracy

Carey's description of communications media in national spaces is useful here, because it distinguishes between the function of technology use in regional spaces and that in national spaces. Carey writes that communications media, "are designed, in an objective sense, to celebrate what unifies the social system, what grounds consensus can be affected upon and not the grounds of irreconcilable differences" (1963, 176).

The Social Credit broadcasts, along with the *Canadian Farm Radio Forum* and *Citizens' Forum* programs, attempted to use radio to discuss the question of post-Depression economic development and postwar reconstruction in a way that allowed for democratic participation and a form of public deliberation on these issues. The case of Alberta radio in the mid-twentieth century reveal the capacity of radio as a deliberative medium. A new technology was used as a coordinating mechanism by which proposed ideas about social development were presented to a mass audience, discussed in small interpersonal groups, after which responses were offered back to the broadcaster. The methods used by Aberhart and Corbett were similar. Both Aberhart and Corbett held well-developed philosophies concerning the relationship of radio to public education. Both used radio as a coordinating technology for small-group discussion. In so doing, the two men developed a regional social field in which the fate of radio broadcasting in Canada was to be played out. In both cases, small study groups had been established that allowed for listeners to meet and discuss the ideas they had heard on the radio and, in turn, to offer back their responses for the consideration of the larger audience. These were experiments in deliberative democracy, using radio as a coordinating technology. The broadcasts of Aberhart and Corbett were complementary to, but also contradictory of, the instrumental rationality that was to be applied to the problem of relief from the Depression and postwar reconstruction and that in fact characterized radio policy itself thereafter.

Though the two approaches to radio were sophisticated and fully conceived, they were, in relation to one another, antipathetic. The deliberative character of the programming of both Aberhart and Corbett flowed from a disillusionment of both men with instrumental rationality as expressed in government policymaking at the time, but for different reasons. Aberhart's view was that the rational choices of society had led it to overlook the economic desperation of many people. Social Credit economic doctrine infused with the compassion of the gospel was the means by which instrumental rationality would be renewed and applied justly. Radio allowed for the introduction of the doctrine. It would allow for the organization of small groups in which the doctrine would be clarified and, to some extent, discussed critically. If individuals were to be mobilized for political action, they had to understand what they had heard and be offered the opportunity to express it one to another. For Aberhart, no discussion meant no action. Corbett, too, believed that social doctrines had to be validated through discussion by those people whom they would affect. His experience as a university teacher suggested that the social context determined to some extent what could be learned. For Corbett, no discussion of ideas meant no validity in context and his view was that Aberhart's broadcasts confounded the ideals of public education. Aberhart was to Corbett's ears bombastic, didactic, and univocal. He describes himself as, "skeptical and slightly contemptuous of the whole undertaking ... on various occasions when storm-bound in some village or farm house I had listened in nervous irritation to [Aberhart's] evangelical bellowing" (Corbett 1957, 51).

Aberhart and Corbett each had a strong relationship with the United Farmers of Alberta (UFA) administration, but the valence of the relationship was different. Until he decided in 1935 to found his own party, Aberhart wanted to use radio to impress on members of the party the wisdom of adopting Social Credit doctrine. His plan was initially to stay out of direct participation in politics but to influence the UFA indirectly through his radio and organizing activities. Eventually, however, the relationship of Aberhart with the UFA became adversarial. Corbett, on the other hand, was a friend of UFA leader Henry Wise Wood and wanted to use radio to raise the fortunes of the UFA after it began its slide in popularity with Wood's retirement in 1931. He approached the UFA Government as a potential ally for developing his radio programs and educational activities. The ideological impetus of each of the two cases was thus quite different. Corbett's programming was based on the philosophy that radio could be used to encourage democratic participation of the public. Aberhart's programming, too, was premised on participation, but it was for a narrower purpose, that of political mobilization and, more specifically, for the "accreditation" of a discrete group of listeners.

The programming of the kind Aberhart and Corbett produced was not unique in Canada. The United Farmers of Ontario experimented with rural radio in the 1937–38, and Macdonald College used a Carnegie Corporation Grant to broadcast to the English-speaking Eastern Townships in Québec (Faris 1975, 87). Similarly, the University of Toronto Extension Department distributed written materials to rural groups listening to a farm radio series in 1935–36, but in that program and others there was no method of providing feedback to the radio talks (Faris 1975, 92). The Alberta developments were early, well organized efforts under the tutelage of two master organizers. The radio broadcasts of Aberhart and Corbett were distinctive, and they attracted national attention.

Though the ideologies of Aberhart and Corbett were different, the results of the contested use of radio in Alberta became part of a similar set of outcomes occurring in different areas of Canada and North America. National identity in Canada was informed by such contests. The strong social identity reflected in the Canadian nation is built up through a kind of regional clearinghouse. Social identity is in this sense always in process within the regional space. The practical expression of culture requires something like pilot projects, many of which appear only briefly before being either left behind or developed further. A few become exemplars for contribution to a strong social identity. The flourishing and decline of the two initiatives was to have an important influence not only on social identity in Alberta, but also on social identity in Canada. The independence from state influence that both cases represents, in addition to the relatively novel methods of deliberation associated with both, can be considered a loss to Canadian culture.

It would be unlikely that radio today could be used in the way it was in the era of Aberhart and Corbett. However, the wide availability of the networked computer in homes across Canada is often identified as offering the potential for deliberative democracy. As the internet may yet do, the broadcasts by Aberhart and Corbett brought ideas, suppositions, arguments, and opinions into a public space. In the case of Aberhart, the desperate situation of farmers and others following the Depression were made "visible" by attempts, through the Social Credit doctrine and to some extent through religious doctrine, to develop a meaningful narrative for social and economic change. That these doctrines were in some ways flawed only points to the desirability to bring them into the open. In the case of Corbett, the direct interference by government in the CBC's programming were revealed through the eventual cancellation of the *Citizens' Forum*.

The deliberative democratic mode of radio developed by Aberhart and Corbett did not prevail. Its contribution to the national cultural pool was that of a dead-end development. Communications technologies would not be a significant part of a process of the deliberating political, cultural, social, or, for that matter religious, ideas in Canada. The two cases suggest that social action, and not technological innovation, will have a decisive influence in the adjudication of those projects engaging the internet as a medium of deliberative democracy.

Conclusion: Radio and Regional Identity

The development of identity in a regional space using technology is illustrated by the case of radio in Alberta. The political tensions that resulted from the radio broadcasts of Aberhart and Corbett provided the first view of the link between regional and national identity. Claxton was a central figure in establishing the link. Beyond these, where is the link between regional technological development in regions and the development of a model of a nationalist logic of organizing in regions? We may consider a comment by Innis, from the conclusion to his history of the Canadian Pacific Railway. Writing in 1923, Innis states that, "Western Canada has paid for the development of Canadian nationality, and it would appear that it must continue to pay. The acquisitiveness of eastern Canada shows little sign of abatement" (reprinted in 1972, 294). Innis saw in the great national technological project of the CPR something of the anchoring regional spaces in which it was actually conceived and made concrete – and which I have described as providing a context for a model of a nationalist logic of organizing in regions.

The first of the premises for the model of a nationalist logic of organizing in regions discussed in the previous chapter involved empirical links from regional cultures to the national culture, observable in *policy and decision-making*. Through the development of radio in Alberta in the 1920s and 1930s, there was a tension introduced between regional and national articulations of social identity. Three results may follow tensions of this kind. They may lie unacknowledged by one or both parties, there may be an unsuccessful attempt to resolve the tension, or the tension may be resolved. The last of these occurred in this case. The regional uses of radio provided an alternative model of radio use, one which was found to be incompatible with national uses. The case reveals the connection between the regional uses of a communications technology and that same technology's ultimate contribution to national social identity as reflected in the national broadcasting policy in 1960 and thereafter. The cultural trajectory that radio adopted in Canada resulted in the content of both radio and television the subject of state regulation for the purpose of maintaining the nation-state's cultural sovereignty.

The regional and national models of broadcasting that now exist are different than they would otherwise have been in the absence of the influence of Aberhart's and Corbett's experiments. In fact, forms of the deliberative model of radio use pioneered by Aberhart and Corbett still exist. CBC Radio's *Cross-Country Checkup* continues as a popular program, although the intensive participation and dialogue characteristic of the earlier programs is absent. Corbett's CKUA still operates, and it is now entirely supported by listeners and available both through broadcast within Alberta and globally through the internet. Similarly, educational broadcasters having their roots in regions, such as TVOntario, have continued to contribute to Canadian cultural life. They also continue to "act back" on national broadcasting systems by providing an alternative to the national model.

The nationalist logic of organizing in the case of radio involved contesting the social meaning of a new technology. Aberhart and Corbett fashioned radio as a tool of deliberative democracy and were able, each in his own way, to position this preferred social meaning in the national discourse about cultural development and social identity. They were able to connect that preferred meaning of the technology to a sense of political cohesion within the region. This political cohesion, especially in the case of Aberhart, was positioned as being in opposition to federal power. This sense of grievance would be taken up by Aberhart's successor, Premier Ernest Manning, in the subsequent decades. The case of radio allows us to view the logic of nationalism in the development of a regional identity through the successive applications of technology. Such a logic at work in the Canadian West is broadly linked to what Laycock (1990) has called the "truly indigenous and distinctive group of democratic political ideologies" that arose in the region during the period between the two world wars of the twentieth century. These ideologies sought the extension of popular democracy in Canada. Radio was an important means by which popular democracy could be enacted. With the advent of radio in the 1920s and the creation of new institutions and organizations in the subsequent decades, new and renewed conversations were initiated about the character of the regional identity and its relationship to the national identity. The deliberative democratic methods of the radio programming of Aberhart and Corbett were followed through to the national development of identity in Canada in the CanCon regulations.

The nationalist logic of organizing in a region that may be observed was therefore opposed to bureaucratic and corporate logics. The case illustrates how at an early stage of a new technology's development, bureaucratic and corporate logics may not be fully developed, offering an opportunity for the expression of diverging social meanings for the technology. The use of radio for deliberation and participation was adjudicated in the national clearinghouse of broadcasting policy in Canada. Technology provided a significant basis for the cultural accommodations required for the nationalist logic of organizing in regional space. The case of radio reveals the connection between the early regional uses of a communications technology and the technology's ultimate contribution to the national broadcasting policy that remains in place.

Examples from other regions in Canada and elsewhere include those instances in which technology has a formative social influence. The K-Net internet initiative is a community networking project in which First Nations are using broadband networks to support community development. Community members use videoconferencing and other technologies to communicate with one another for the purpose of cultural, social, and economic development (Walmark 2005). The regional council is called Keewaytinook Okimakanak, which means "Northern Chiefs" in Oji-Cree. It serves Deer Lake, Fort Severn, Keewaywin, McDowell Lake, North Spirit Lake, and Poplar Hill First Nations. The organization is directed by the chiefs of the member First Nations. The council advises and assists its First Nations in such areas as health, education, economic development, employment assistance, legal, public works, finance and administration, and computer communications (K-Net Services). K-Net Services supports email, online bulletin board, and cultural development through personal webpages. As these technologies are used there are *intra*community linkages but also intercommunity linkages. Networking for their own purposes has led to more relationships with other First Nations groups but also with the provincial and federal governments and other community networks across Canada. By adopting broadband technologies, the member First Nations become more deeply embedded with other communities and regional identities in Canada.

In the case of radio in Alberta, technology provided the medium by which the modern character of regional and national identities was developed. In the case we see that *technological practices in regional spaces influence those in national spaces.* Technology in this sense may be viewed as a "first fact" in the sequence of events within the nationalist logic of organizing. The meaning of technology in the development of regional and national identities is primarily that of modernization. Its capacity for democratic participation within the nationalist project is constructed by actors working within two social dynamics: that of technology and nationalism, and that of region and nation.

5

THE DEMONSTRATION EFFECT
AND THE SOCIAL MEANING
OF NEW ORGANIZATIONS

> The fact that struggles over identity... concern
> the imposition of perceptions and categories of
> perception helps to explain the decisive place
> which, like the strategy of the *manifesto* in artis-
> tic movements, *the dialectic of manifestation or
> demonstration* holds in all regionalist or nation-
> alist movements.
>
> Bourdieu 1991, 224;
> emphasis in the original

Innovation and occupational mobility may be considered measures of economic growth. Through innovation and occupational mobility, industrial societies increase their production, share of markets, and economic output. They increase the standard of living for members of the society, providing a signal of the potential benefits of the nationalist project and a view of the economic, political, and social effects of achieving the political condition of "one state, one culture." Both innovation and occupational mobility are more potent in their social meaning the closer they are to the urgent and proximate concerns of the population.

Innovation is seeing anew. Seeing anew involves forgetting something of the old, if only for a moment, in anticipation of the moment when the new becomes the familiar. Both social innovation and technological innovation therefore require forgetting. New ideas must first be anchored in existing cultural knowledge, after which they are rendered more familiar, less "strange." Innovation involves untethering social relations from the present time and place, from what is familiar, to new relations in some future that has to this point seemed obscure. Finally the new ideas become old ideas. They become objective fact. In the words of Hobsbawm (Hobsbawm and Ranger 1983), this is the moment of the "invention of tradition," when the national culture takes on the quality of immemoriality. Innovation means that things will not stay the same. In the parlance of the local politician seeking re-election, citizens of the prospective nation-state are asked to vote for a change. The message is particularly attractive to people moving from rural areas to urban centres. But it is equally of interest to white-collar workers in the cities for whom growth translates into the incremental rise in salary. Innovation is both process and product, but it is the product that has political uses for the nationalist, because an "innovation as product" has demonstrational potential.

Occupational mobility, like innovation, is a prerequisite for economic growth. It becomes a tangible benefit of the nationalist program for individuals and groups. Occupational mobility is a sort of innovation, in that it is a product of new social and technological relations. It must be established at the regional level if individuals are to recognize and experience it as deeply relevant to their concerns and engage it as such. Van den Bossche (2003) points to such messages as political cartoons as evidence that a nationalist dialogue has occurred between elite and the larger population. Political cartoons represent an illustrative, literally pictorial, view of the new world through the lens of the newspaper. In addition to the quite concrete messages of political cartoons and other popular expressions of political dialogue, there are more abstract yet no less powerful bodies of messages about the nationalist project.

This chapter examines two mechanisms or methods by which innovation and occupational mobility are achieved in regional and national spaces. First, in creating or encouraging the creation of the sociotechnology of a new organization, the state is shown to be active, potent, and engaged. New organizations in the nationalist state may be private or public in ownership and operation, or some hybrid of the two. The state may create the organization, or there may be some collaboration between state and the private realm. Yet all organizations are subject to the regulation of the state, and all demonstrate the emerging relationship of national culture and the productivity of the national state. All provide both symbolic and material wealth to a population. The symbol of the new organization is that of growth and advancement – for both the nation and the individual. Being a member of the nation means sharing, at some level and in some measure, the national wealth. The material benefits of new organizations include new jobs and the promise, if not always fulfilled, of an increase in the gross domestic product. An aerospace program – in Canada as much as in the US or in Indonesia – may become part of the national culture in the regional allocation of jobs, through the local manufacturing and service activities to which it gives rise.

Second, by encouraging the adoption of new technology, the nationalist project contributes to and thereby remains a member of the global technological club. National pride is increased when technology is used to accomplish economic goals. The pursuit of these goals may occur in regional contexts to reduce the risk of failure in national spaces. Or they may provide symbolic and material evidence of the benefits of the nationalist logic of organizing. The demonstration effect its relevance to nationalism is discussed in the next section, following which the case of a new organization's character as a demonstration effect is presented.

The Demonstration Effect and Nationalism

The demonstration effect (see chapter 3, above) is important for sustaining national ideas and culture, because it contributes a common rhetorical thread for the people involved in the nationalist project (Gellner 1965). In this chapter, we see the example of a new organization whose mandate and mission were connected to those state economic priorities whose symbolic function constituted a demonstration effect within the region.

The theory of the diffusion of innovations has developed increasingly complex models of the adoption of technologies and other innovations, including social innovations. The basic principle of the diffusion of innovations is that the messages of mass media alone cannot account for the adoption of a technological or social innovation. Instead, potential adopters seek interpersonal sources, such as friends and family members, as sources of expertise and experience. Diffusion of innovations therefore posits a two-step flow of, first, message receipt through a media channel, and, second, validation of the message through interpersonal communication (Rogers 1995). The earliest instances of the two-step flow have been noted in history not in the twentieth century but four hundred years earlier in the decades following the invention of the printing press. Köhler describes the process in the sixteenth century whereby evangelical teachers read newly published works, which were made available by the many independent printing houses, and then spread the ideas contained in them orally to those who could not read. The two-step flow helps to explain "how illiterate people could participate in a communication process, which relied on a printed medium (or – for that matter – how the content of Latin texts could have been passed on to the vast majority of the population, who did not understand that language)" (Köhler 1986, 164).

Following the two-step flow theory, the demonstration effect suggests that technology "teaches" by becoming an exemplar of the benefits of nationalism. The demonstration effect is mediated through technology, and its subject is technology. Technological innovation is used as a means of publicly illustrating the material and social advantages that a nationalist project offers individuals and groups. By creating "news" about the innovations inherent in a nationalist project, the demonstration effect stimulates face-to-face conversations about the project. It is important for sustaining a nationalist ideology, because it provides the continuing and unifying rhetorical thread for the many individuals and groups involved in the nationalist project (Gellner 1965). It reveals the benefits for individuals and groups participating in the nationalist project.

Technology, including the sociotechnological innovation of a new organization, represents the symbolic scope of nationalism. The demonstration effect is a didacticism. It "teaches" a lesson about the future of the nation in relation to a nationalist project. It portrays the hitherto abstract prospects of the nation in the practical terms of a world of nations. Technology teaches about the nationalist project by representing the symbolic scope of nationalism. Technology is a core feature of modernism, and the kind of nationalism that is on offer is one that will be organized technocratically. A reformed educational system, for example, will make use of modern methods of organization, including the professionalization of teachers, the creation for and by them of a body of professional knowledge, and the granting of the powers of professional self-governance. Through the demonstration effect, technology illustrates and enumerates the benefits available to members of the nation. A nationalized petrochemical company, or a state-supported effort to socialize the benefits of the natural or cultural resources of the nation, promises some portion of the income from such resources for citizens, blue-collar jobs for nationals, and, of particular interest to intellectual elites, white-collar jobs and the development of an upper middle-class.

Nationalism is led by political and social elites, but it requires the mobilization of a large number of people. The nationalist project is made attractive for populations by a surplus of benefits over disadvantages. Individuals accept certain sacrifices in making cultural accommodations that represent support for or acquiescence in the homogenous culture of the nationalist project. They must feel that such compromises and adjustment will have the effect of improving their day-to-day lives. The demonstration effect is a means by which a population comes to understand and engage with the material promises of the nationalist project.

The demonstration effect may be rooted in a distant part of the world. A consequence of such an event is that a nationalist movement is provided with a view of what is possible in its own part of the world. Alternatively, the demonstration effect may be found in the homeland of the nationalist project.

Technology and nationalism are related through more than the hardware and software of communications technologies and mass media, more also than the real estate and equipment of manufacturing plants and repair shops. Technology includes the administrative structures by which social, political, and economic projects are pursued. The case of the creation of Nova Corporation in Alberta in 1954, a company created to gather petroleum from within the province for export, illustrates the demonstration effect as an expression of the nationalist logic of organizing that is active in a region. It shows how the political and economic interests of individuals and groups within a regional polity may converge in the logic of nationalism as it is enacted within a region. Through the lens of nationalism, we can see the mutual relationship of ideas and technology in regional economic and political development that we would otherwise be unable to do. When viewed as a modern phenomenon, nationalism is preceded by the development and dissemination of new ideas about technology, in particular ideas about its capacity to reconfigure large segments of society. The process of fashioning "strange" ideas about technology into "familiar" ones must involve, in turn, the use of technologies of media and communication. New organizations are concrete entities and make aspects of the regional identity visible, through their outputs of services or products, and also through the economic implications for communities. They are emblematic of growth, symbolizing the capacity of the state to accomplish something.

New organizations and technology adoption are, in summary, an important means by which the demonstration effect occurs. The demonstration effect is both symbolic and didactic, as the case in this chapter illustrates. It can reveal the practices of a nationalist logic of organizing and the ways that this logic is combined with corporate and bureaucratic logics. In particular, the following practice may be observed: that of establishing the citizen as a consumer and shareholder of state enterprises.

Nova Corporation and the Demonstration Effect

In 1935, the Social Credit Party of Alberta defeated the incumbent United Farmers of Alberta Party and formed a provincial government that would be re-elected continuously until 1971, an unusually consistent pattern for a Canadian province. In its first two decades in power, the Social Credit Government was riven by the question of how to fulfill its capacity to act decisively. In the first few years after its founding, the Social Credit Party never had a shortage of ideas. It was the linking of these ideas to a coherent and recognizable political program of action that put up limits to the government's capacity to maintain political support. The establishment of Nova Corporation in 1954 was the first in a series of decisions that reflected the recognition that establishing or acquiring new organizations could demonstrate a capacity to act. The new company would become the first among many efforts over the decades since then supporting the explanatory description provided here of a new organization functioning to demonstrate the benefits for individuals of continued affinity for a regional social identity.

Social Credit was a populist political party that emerged quickly in a sparsely populated hinterland region. Innis notes that regional parties in Canada have "enjoyed the prestige which attaches to ideas imported from Great Britain" (Innis 1995, 273). The party was founded on the basis of ideas developed in middle-class England, the home of its founder, Major Clifford H. Douglas. Ideology is communicated according to both its intellectual underpinning and the public project with which it becomes popularly associated. Nova Corporation was established during a period in which the party's emerging ideological framework combined with a nascent agenda for political action. This agenda would eventually become recognized as a succession of public projects demonstrating the economic and political potency of the ideology of regionalism. The chronology of events by which the ideas of Social Credit were expressed in action began in 1935, with the promises made during the election campaign that year: "Aberhart offered the people a programme of social action. Social Credit, a *subjective* system of ideas, could become, through human effort, the *objective* economic and social reality" (Irving 1959, 264).

Sagging grain prices, Depression, and Prairie drought, which were more conventional explanations for the province's poverty, were rejected as possible causes by the Social Crediters. Instead, following the Douglasite analysis, Aberhart claimed that there was a basic flaw in the Canadian monetary system. Large businesses, especially those based in Central Canada, had the "ability to create financial credit without costs and to pass the costs of intermediary production on to the people as prices without an equivalent sum provided through wages" (Hesketh 1997, 53–4). There was an imbalance in the supply of purchasing power that left citizens in a "deficit" position. According to Social Credit theory, the deficit between business credit and the capacity of the population to purchase goods could be filled by "social credit," scrip that would be issued to citizens. Aberhart called for monetary reform, basic dividends for citizens, and the "just" price of goods and services. Citizens could have a role in demanding reform of the financial system, but for this to happen government would need to sharpen its conception of its constituency. In the Social Credit view as adopted in Alberta, there were no citizens, in fact, only consumers. The following is a summary in the *Calgary Herald* in February of a speech by Aberhart in 1933: "The basic idea is that all citizens of a country own its natural resources and are entitled to a share in their distribution, instead of permitting a few financiers to exploit them. From this it follows that a government must function for the benefit of all citizens instead of favoring privileged classes, whether manufacturers, producers, or bankers. Every citizen is a consumer and so the consumer must be the first consideration of a government" (Irving 1959, 58).

People in the province developed the expectation that the election of the government in 1935 would result in immediate, tangible benefits for individuals. These benefits were not simply election promises, although there had been specific promises made; rather, the benefits were entwined with the new ideology that the Social Credit had promulgated. Yet neither the aspiring nor elected government stated what the benefits would actually be. This created a tension in the government's attempts to develop its political program. Both before and after the election, Aberhart and Douglas had difficulty translating their complex economic analysis into a practical program of political action. At times, the potential powerlessness of a Social Credit Government came to the surface. Douglas, who visited in Alberta in March 1934 to discuss the political prospects for creating a Social Credit Government in Alberta, was asked to explain the application of his ideas in a province in which banking was expressly not within the government's power. He avoided the question for the first part of his visit but toward the end of it admitted, "If you have no powers, then of course you cannot do anything" (Irving 1959, 89). In response to a growing expectation that the government would be able to deliver a substantive economic or social benefit to Albertans, Aberhart had promised in the election a $25 "basic dividend." However, even this turned out to be a phantom. With this failure of action, there was some rationalization that needed to be done by supporters of the government in the years after the initial election victory. Reporting on his interviews with Alberta citizens, Irving notes that

> [t]he more prosperous farmers and small-town business men who became Social Crediters almost invariably deny that they were at all influenced by the prospect of basic dividends. They add that they certainly never expected to receive them. They frequently go out of their way to explain that Aberhart used the "suggestion" of $25 monthly merely as a figure of speech, for the purpose of "illustrating" what *might* be achieved under a proper monetary system. But, after making this apology, they usually admit that the poor farmers and small-town business men, as well as the lower middle and working classes, were completely taken in by the promise of $25 monthly, and really believed that Aberhart would secure it for them. (1959, 249–50)

No tangible benefits – no public projects – could be identified in the government's first term of office, in spite of the ethereal promises. This created a loss of some public support over the next number of years, though the Alberta public was patient, re-electing the government after the discovery in 1947 of massive oil reserves in the province. It was only a few years after this discovery that the provincial ownership of natural resources was recognized by the Social Credit Government as a possible avenue for applying its doctrine of delivering an economic benefit to the "consumers" of Alberta. From 1947, the year of the first significant discovery of oil at Leduc, the government began to adapt some of the Social Credit ideas in a way that would suit the rosy economic and political possibilities of the nascent era of oil. It began to promote the notion that the relationship between citizen and government was comparable to that between consumer and retail seller and that this conception could inform a broad political agenda:

> The Social Crediters... conceived democracy in the image of a business system, but, more up to date than [their predecessors, the

United Farmers of Alberta, who governed between 1921 and 1934],
their image was that of a giant corporation, in which the shareholders are atomized, their voices reduced to proxies, and their
effective rights reduced to the one right of receiving a dividend…
In the later stages of Social Credit thinking, even the model of the
business corporation was discarded as savouring too much of majority rule, only to be replaced by another commercial image, the
relation of seller and buyer in the retail market—an even more fragmented relation than that of directors and shareholders. (Macpherson 1953, 233)

When it was established, the control of Nova Corporation, initially
named Alberta Gas Trunk Line, was vested among Alberta's utilities,
gas processors, exporting companies, and the provincial government
itself. Non-voting shares were sold to Alberta residents. The company
would build, own, and operate a provincewide natural gas transportation that would be the largest company of its kind in Canada. Nova
would also open a kind of window on the industry for the provincial
government, much in the same way Petro-Canada did for the federal
government in the 1970s. By 1979, Nova had become the seventh largest
company operating in Western Canada, with annual sales of $1.24 bil-
lion and assets of $3.1 billion (Biggest and best 1980, 12).

The Alberta Government established structural and symbolic insti-
tutional linkages with Nova Corporation that functioned reciprocally.
Structurally, the company was governed by a system that included
public representation. Provincial legislation provided both positive
and negative direction for the company's operations. The company
would have a monopoly on gathering natural gas for export, but it
could not become involved in other businesses. Symbolically, the
company helped to underline popular ideas being promoted by the
government that involved strengthening the province's substantive
ownership of natural resources. Also symbolically, the company was
connected to the regulatory regime set up by the Alberta Government
to entrench the explicit economic and political interests that the
province held in resource ownership. With the establishment of Nova
Corporation, a set of government priorities was reflected in the demonstration effect. These priorities envisioned the essential threat to the

interests of small producers to be *not* the US ownership of the means of production but the Central Canadian claim on the economic development of the resource. After the Nova Corporation experience, future provincial governments in Alberta would engage in a diverse range of other investments as a means of enhancing provincial political and economic autonomy. The institutions and organizations established or purchased to contribute to this program, all during the 1970s, included Pacific Western Airlines, Alberta Energy Company, a provincial share of Syncrude Canada Ltd, and the Alberta Petroleum Marketing Commission.

For a conservative government in a mainly rural province in the 1950s, the dramatic action of creating a private company would need to be supported by socially legitimated ideas. The tight coupling of an organization's constitution and operations to a central sociopolitical process could not be undertaken without an ideological account of the need for such an action. The public, as well as key actors and groups, would need to be motivated to support and carry out the task. The ideology of regionalism provided such a rationale, which was characterized in two ways: by the ideas themselves, and by the public project (the demonstration effect) by which these ideas were enacted.

Nova Corporation was the first organization in the province to demonstrate what the developing regionalist identity would mean in practice for individuals and groups in the province. The new organization's structure allowed not only provincial influence over the company, which indirectly meant control of natural resources but also the opportunity for Albertans to purchase and own shares in the company. The notion of Aberhart's "basic dividend" of $25 was finally fulfilled symbolically in Nova Corporation. The sale of company shares was congruent with the government's conception of the relation of citizens to the state as that of consumer and retail seller. The demonstration effect of establishing the company made explicit the benefits of regionalism. In turn, the company was to become viewed as a legitimate entity not only within the province but across Canada. No greater legitimacy is available to an organization than the state's grant of exclusive access to a market, and Nova Corporation received such a grant. The social identity to which Nova contributed was a membership implied in the economic and political benefits for individuals and groups that were available in the political agenda of regionalism and which were made visible in the demonstration effect of public projects such as Nova Corporation. The establishment of the company provided economic and political support for the state by maintaining a monopoly of regional private interests in opposition to external, mainly Central Canadian, interests.

The fledgling Nova had the explicit purpose of gathering and distributing natural gas in a web of thousands of kilometres of underground pipelines within the province. The company also had an implicit function, which was to support the goals of economic and political integration under the umbrella of an emerging regionalism. Nova's overt purpose was the avoidance of foreign control of gas exports. Foreign control refers to powers outside the geographic region of the province, but mainly Eastern Canadian interests. The Social Credit Government ensured that Nova would not be allowed to contract with gas exporters, because of a fear that indirect control of the company would fall into the hands of outsiders. The company would be confined exclusively to the business of gathering and transmitting gas. It would not have the full monopoly power of a public utility but neither would it have the freedom of operation and ownership of a private corporation. The initial sales of the shares show that the gathering and sale of natural gas from the province was to be carried out by a monopoly of private interests, including some of the world's largest petroleum producers. The provincial government reinforced this monopoly by creating a regulatory institution that functions to this day to mediate the operations of gas producers and buyers. The Alberta Energy and Utilities Board (formerly the Alberta Energy Resources Conservation Board) regulates shipments of natural gas.

A shift had begun after World War II in Alberta that saw the relative proportion of the rural and urban populations change entirely. While in the 1930s the rural population had accounted for roughly three-quarters of the population, by the 1960s it would account for only about a quarter of the population. Periods of social reorganization and transformation are fertile for nationalist movements, because it is at these times that the need is felt to address the grievances of a large group of economically or socially disadvantaged individuals (Gellner 1965, 1983). State-building during these periods is associated with a legitimate mode of sponsorship, an umbrella under which the interests of economic and political elites, with the support of the polity, engage in a program of economic and political integration. In Canada, federalism reflects the regional nature of state-building, which is rooted, in turn, in regional economic activity.

Although industrialization in Canada has to some degree displaced a reliance on the natural resources on which regional economic activity is based, regionalism remains an important influence within the Canadian political economy. The province of Alberta in the 1950s was in social and economic transition. Agriculture and coal-mining, which had been the major industries until the Second World War, were giving way to the new era of oil. During the same period of time, the proportion of people living in cities steadily increased and those in rural areas decreased. In 1957 the last of the Galt Mines closed, and by 1964 the Shaughnessy Mines of Lethbridge Colleries was shut down. Yet the Social Credit Government's political constituency during the 1950s was these same farmers, coal-miners, and small producers whose political influence was now reduced. The political and economic benefits of the oil wealth were seen to flow to the federal government in Ottawa. Caldarola argues that the conflict between the two regions of Canada was so strong that decades later it resulted in a formative effect on social structure: "[T]he struggle between the West and the East has taken on such importance in people's minds that class antagonisms within the province are dampened" (1979, 195).

During the 1950s, the Social Credit, relying on a homespun version of imported political ideas and with its support mainly from the predominantly rural population, was only glimpsing the economic and political changes that were likely to accompany the era of oil. Nova Corporation contributed to a hierarchical arrangement of organizations and interests in the oil and gas industry and throughout the province more widely. It would be an autonomous company, but it would carry a leading role in enacting the provincial government's intent to prevent a monopsony (a monopoly of central Canadian buyers of the commodity). Other oil and gas companies – created either before or after 1954 – would be required to recognize the explicit role of Nova in representing the government's interest in ensuring an orderly development of the natural gas sector. The government would have indirect leverage in monitoring the supply of natural gas in response to demand.

Regional Identity in Alberta

A distinct challenge for those trying to understand and describe regional identity in Canada is that ethnic and linguistic characteristics, as distinguishing differences in relation to other regions, cannot be established clearly. Recent popular attempts to elaborate on Alberta's social identity, for example, scrutinize opinions about Alberta's regional identity as expressed by those living outside of Alberta, based on errors in fact, as well as generalizations and stereotypes (Ford 2005; Sharpe et al. 2005). Although the Alberta provincial state has in its century-long history sought many of the same political and economic goals of a fully developed nationalism, the ideology associated with its regime has been a variation of a nationalist identity, as may be used to describe, for example, Scottish nationalism or Québec nationalism. While the Québécois may refer to their "way of life" as a means of distinguishing their national culture from Central Canadian values, Albertans cannot. Holding the same largely Protestant, English-speaking values as those of Central Canada, some other means of expressing their discontent was required. Regionalism provided that means. Regionalism in Alberta has operated along the industrial and economic fissures (the uneven impact of industrialization) that are fundamental to nationalist movements. Without regionalism, the popular sentiment needed to hold aloft such actions as creating a provincially sponsored private corporation could not find expression. There was no unifying ethnic, religious, or linguistic coherence in the development of Alberta regionalism, only a strong sense of political alienation aligned with a regional set of economic grievances. The situation was complicated by the cultural diversity that has characterized a region founded on immigration. At the time of the election of the Social Credit Government in Alberta in 1935, "Alberta was considerably over-represented among those of East European and Scandinavian descent, with location quotients considerably over two. Ethnic diversity was clearly a significant feature of western Canadian social structure and particularly of pre-Social Credit Alberta" (Hiller 1977, 63).

In Alberta in 1941, there was "considerable class homogeneity among the independent agrarian producers, but there was also considerable ethnic heterogeneity among the newly arrived residents of Alberta" (Hiller 1977, 64). In his famous analysis of Alberta political economy,

Macpherson (1953) stated that the Alberta of the first four decades of the twentieth century provided a welcoming political climate for a radical doctrine such as that of the Social Credit, because the province was characterized by the frustrations and aspirations of a relatively homogeneous population that was united by its subordination to the outside economy. Macpherson referred to this as Alberta's "predominantly small-propertied basis," observing that the Social Credit was one of a series of radical political movements in the province that was shaped by the region's economic and political subordination to the more mature Canadian economy.

The most radical of the movements in the province has been, of course, political separatism from the Canadian federation. As mentioned in chapter 3, the two antecedents for separatism are a change in the economic horizon and a disturbance in the symbolic order. When these two antecedents are combined, there is the potential for a new ideology, which is fuelled by alienation (identified by Hiller as the negative part of the ideology) and boosterism (the positive part of the ideology). The need for ethnic homogeneity as a unifying influence in the polity disappears, because "peripheral status substitutes for ethnic status as the basis for regional identity in the western regions of Australia and Canada" (Hiller 1987b, 39). It is not surprising, then, that ownership of natural resources and technological development become the subject of ideological accounts seeking secession: "The general content of the western regional ideology is that the concentration of political and economic power in another more dominant region has thwarted peripheral western development, and has generally relegated the west to a marginal position within the wider society" (ibid., 49).

Hiller's analysis would suggest that Macpherson's explanation having to do with homogeneity of the population as an explanatory factor for the success of the Social Credit movement is insufficient. Much of Social Credit's success had to do with accommodation and participation of a diverse population. Similarly, Bell argues that Macpherson's characterization of Social Credit as a petit-bourgeois (small producers) movement is inaccurate and was never supported by empirical examination. Electoral support in 1935, for example, was high in the four largest cities: Edmonton (37 percent), Calgary (58 percent), Lethbridge (53 percent), and Medicine Hat (62 percent).

More recently, the actions of the Alberta Government to organize the efforts of individuals and groups has been identified as a form of corporatism (Harrison 1995). Panitch (1979) defines corporatism as follows: "A universal scheme of vocational, industrial or sectoral organization, whereby the constituent units would have the right of representation in national decision-making, and a high degree of functional autonomy, but would have the duty of maintaining the functional hierarchy and social discipline consistent with the needs of the nation-state as a whole" (119).

Corporatism is a strategy associated with a particular period of time. The Alberta Government of the 1990s has been referred to as a corporatist state, because it encouraged the creation of various non-competitive associations, whose interests were organized hierarchically (Kachur and Harrison 1999; Taft 1999). This conception of corporatism is in harmony with Schmitter's definition (1993), which is that corporatism is "one of several possible arrangements through which interest associations can intermediate between their members (individuals, families, firms, groups of all kinds) and their interlocutors (especially agencies of the state with authority and other resources to satisfy their demands)" (196).

While corporatism provides a useful map of state action in concert with representatives of elite organizations, it does not describe, as the model of a nationalist logic of organizing in regions does, the fully ideological basis for the state's actions, especially as these actions are consistently supported by the polity over a period of decades. The corporatist account does not explain the motivations for social integration that drive state action. Corporatism relies instead on a basic desire of the populace for order and coherence. Social identity in the regionalist account provides a common basis not only for the legitimation of state action but for the wider process of social integration. Without recourse to ethnicity, religion, or language as a distinguishing characteristic for a social identity, public economic projects show how membership in the regional or provincial polity can be different in kind from membership in other polities.

The demonstration effect serves to encourage social integration through the development of a social identity. Regionalism is in part an economic phenomenon in that widely accruing economic benefits are shown to be manifestly available to individuals, especially as these individuals are established as clients or consumers in relation to the state. It is attached to economic activities as a practice, but it is not essentially economic in nature. It transcends the economic because of its ideological nature. Unlike the strategies of province-building and corporatism, regionalism provides a basis for analyzing the ideological basis for those state actions that are intended to accomplish economic and political integration. It establishes a broad basis of consensus regarding the appropriateness of the state's interests.

In Alberta, public projects related to resource development, and which are in support of an increase of provincial autonomy, have had particular ideological value in relation to regionalism. The case of Nova Corporation illustrates the demonstration effect, showing how the political and economic interests of individuals and groups within the regional polity could converge.

Conclusion: The Social Meaning of New Organizations

The practices associated with the nationalist logic of organizing in a region that were presented in this chapter involved establishing a certain relationship between the individual and the state. The individual as a consumer has a shareholder's relationship to the state and a material and symbolic stake in the state's economic activities. The state shifts its economic priorities in ways that entrench its role as the producer, rather than allocator, of wealth.

Nova Corporation became an important part of the regional identity of the West (Richards and Pratt 1979). Over the four decades of its operation, the company functioned as a symbol of a regional determination to maintain a stake in the exploitation of its natural resources. Nova was the largest company in Alberta for many years and was one of the handful of the largest companies in the Canadian West. It maintained a high-profile presence in many Alberta communities through its regional offices and its corporate support for community activities. The company formally loosened its connection to the Alberta Government, diversifying into petrochemical processing across the continent in the 1990s. Plants in Alberta, Ontario, and the US were built or purchased as part of Nova's corporate diversification efforts. Nova Corporation was purchased by TransCanada Pipelines in 1998.

The case of a new organization that had an important formative social influence on both region and nation has its counterpart in other organizations in Canada. Nova Corporation was created in a way that reflected the regional political economy during the period of transformation following the Leduc oil discovery of 1947. It shaped regional identity to the extent that it reflected the parallel intentions of the Alberta Government to maintain a strong hand in the exploitation of a natural resource (in response to potential encroachments by the federal government), while maintaining the conditions under which private ownership of production were ensured. There are other examples of how such development of social identity occurs in a region. Friesen (2000) describes the local culture in Ontario that has drawn on changed local conceptions of time and space. He suggests that a key aspect of regional culture is financial insecurity in the midst of wealth and plenty. The continuous improvement required of workers, along with the demands of balancing home and work, is part of the contemporary experience for "Frank" and his family. In addition, although both company and community are relatively affluent, the fear of job loss haunts the daily lives of Frank and his co-workers. Clock-time and "insecurity in plenty" are linked by Friesen to the transformations of print-capitalism to what he calls "screen capitalism." He argues that the meaning of the organization is to be found in the changes in life-chances and opportunities for social and economic exchange for individuals.

I have suggested that the meaning of an organization must include recognition of its implications for regional identity. Imperial Oil was from its founding in 1880, in London, Ontario, a company that relied for its corporate ethos on the personal example of its founder, Frederick Fitzgerald (Hayes 1988). Until the 1980s, Fitzgerald's example was used within the company as a model for employee development, instilling the Southern Ontario values of thrift, independence, and personal integrity. It has been an Ontario company to much the same degree that Nova was an Alberta company, expressing the meaning of being a resident of that region in terms that are rooted in the local and regional political economy.

There are other examples suggesting that within nationalist projects that are successful in their objective of creating their own state, a population of regional projects is in constant motion. The resulting "pool" contains potential adopters of technology, and the adoption of technology among individuals and groups, including groups within a national polity. Such cases as the one described in this chapter suggest that the demonstration effect provides a concrete example of the benefits and outcomes of the nationalist project. However, the demonstration effect may be rooted in local and regional concerns. *Nationalist organizing is therefore accomplished in part through a regional logic.*

The demonstration effect, the use of symbolic events based on material shifts in the political economy, is an important means by which cultural diversity has been accommodated within regional identities in Canada. It should be noted that in comparison with other nation-states, Canada's federated political structure involves decentralization of powers to the provincial order of government that would be unusual in another country. The applicability of the regional paradigm may be limited to political economies in which some significant powers may be exercised. What remains to be explored is the appropriateness of the nationalist paradigm in other regional contexts in Canada in which alienation is not as conspicuous a part of the political culture.

6

THE INTERNET AND THE FUTURE OF TECHNOLOGY AND NATIONALISM

> To be a Canadian is to adjust to the inevitable contingency of the nation itself.
>
> Friesen 2000, 224–5

In 2002, the National Broadband Task Force published its final report (Government of Canada 2002). Established two years earlier, the task force had been charged by the federal government with creating a new vision for Canada as a broadband-enabled nation. The report presented a comprehensive vision of a nation that would be connected by the new communications medium of the internet. Communities large and small across the vast expanse of Canada would have access to the internet's services and diversions. The report used the language familiar from previous ages of the rhetoric of technological nationalism: the telegraph and railroad lines of the nineteenth century, the national radio and television service of the 1930s and 1940s, and satellite communications of the 1970s. It recommended that all communities have access to the internet: "We believe, as a matter of urgency, that all Canadians should have access to broadband network services so that they can live and prosper in any part of the land and have access to high levels of education, health, cultural and economic opportunities" (Government of Canada 2002, 9).

Beyond a small number of pilot projects, the universal internet access contemplated by the report has not been pursued, except in Alberta. The Alberta SuperNet project, completed in 2005, connects 429 communities across the vast territory of the region. In each of these communities, the schools, hospitals, government offices, and public libraries have been connected to broadband services (Province of Alberta 2006). As with many other large-scale construction projects in the region's history, this one combined public and private capital. The base network, which serves some of the larger towns and cities, is owned by Bell Canada, while the provincial government owns the rest of the network, which is operated by a private contractor. The province also stipulated that the basic charge for carrying telecommunications services were to be the same across the province, whether in metropolitan centres or the remote and sparsely populated areas of the north. Albertans are to be "more connected than ever."

The internet is the most recent media innovation in history by which the relationship of technology to nationalism may be assessed. Using the historical perspective adopted in previous chapters, this final chapter explores possible futures for regional technological development and its relationship to nationalism. Within a succession of media "punctuations" in history, the internet builds cumulatively on the effects of previous media. Also in common with older media, the internet's appearance represents a break with the effects of previous media. The internet's social meaning in connection to nationalism is related to its capacity to connect the user at once to the culture of the local and the global, as well as to those of the regional and the national. As Carey points out, "[i]t was a widespread notion in the 1990s that Internet technology was a force in globalization, creating borderless worlds and borderless communities, borderless organizations and borderless politics. There is truth in that generalization. But what is equally true, is that as one set of borders, one set of social structures, is taken down, another set of borders is erected" (Carey 2005, 453).

To examine such disjunctures, along with continuities, the modernizing effects of the internet are discussed in this chapter. Then the internet's developing relationship with a nationalist logic of organizing will be considered in the following ways: the technology's convergent character, the phenomenon of "glocalism" revealed by internet use and its contribution to heterogenous social identities, the internet as a sort of national culture in itself, and the increasing use of the internet by diaspora communities. Some reflections on the historical connection between region and nation are provided as a conclusion.

Modernizing Effects of Technologies in History

Technology is at the centre of the modern project of nationalism. It will continue to figure prominently in those historical and sociological accounts in which nationalism is regarded as a feature of modernity and in which industrialization is considered to be a significant explanatory factor for the emergence and spread of nationalism. The use of technology to enable the wide circulation of new ideas about social identity within a society gives life to a nationalist project. Indeed, the spread of nationalism has relied on the increasingly mediated character of modern communications. Modern political messages are never exchanged directly between politician and the *polis* but between politician and mass audience, through the enabling channel of communications technologies and through technologies' demonstration effect. Because the mass media are subject to control by individuals and small groups, the spread of nationalism, too, is subject to hegemonic control. For this reason, Habermas (1996) points out that nationalism is inherently susceptible to manipulation and abuse by political elites. The cultural context in which appeals to nationalist sentiment are made will therefore continue to be of interest to scholars of technology and nationalism. Studies of nationalism in their cultural context that use both qualitative and quantitative inquiry, poetry and statistics, firsthand accounts, and theoretical reflections can demonstrate the complexity and richness of the increasingly mediated social world of emerging and developing nationalist projects. Such interdisciplinary accounts may allow us to see more clearly when and in what circumstances members of political elites find it possible to mobilize popular sentiment in support of nationalism and under what conditions the nationalist strategy is likely to succeed.

Paradoxically, technology animates the national project in part by mediating the tension between modernity and antimodernity through the capacity to revive dead or dying linguistic variants and to give new cultural life to forgotten texts and artifacts. It provides the tools needed for the invention of national traditions through the admonition to the citizens of a nation to "remember." The ideological tension between modernity and antimodernity within the nationalist project comes to be concerned with social progress, and this allows for its continued development over time.

As we have seen, technology and the Canadian nation-state have developed interdependently. In the modern age of technology, nationalist discourse has concerned itself with the capacities of technology to shape the identity of the modern citizen. The rhetorical uses of technology for the development of social identity in Canada – from railroad to radio and television broadcasting, and then to the internet – have emerged in connection to the discursive development of modernity. Canadian social identity in a world of nations has been described in terms of two possibilities. In one view, technology is a historical and continuing threat to the nationalist project. A reliance on tradition – and in particular a subjective but historically constituted social identity – provides the legitimate basis for national unity. Such unity is seen to be undermined by technology's totalizing and universalizing qualities. A contrasting view is the more liberal and by far the most widely articulated and accepted of the two. In this view, technology is properly used to facilitate the aims of a national social identity. In their understanding and use of technology, citizens of the nation continually expand the legitimate basis of the nation-state, a legitimacy in which cultural plurality enjoys an overriding moral authority.

Along a continuum between these poles of idealism and pragmatism have developed the various regional expressions and enactments of the nationalist logic of organizing. I have argued that the idealist and pragmatist strains of thought about technology in Canada are the product of cultural activity in both regional and national spaces. The model of a nationalist logic of organizing in regions that I have presented suggests that cultural development in Canada takes place within a pool of potential, emerging, and substantive contributions to national culture. An empirical link was shown between regional aspirations regarding radio broadcasting and the eventual policy adjudication of the uses of that technology at the national level. The demonstration effect associated with technology in the development of nationalism was illustrated through the case of a provincial government's creation of a new organization whose contribution to the regional social identity was connected to the capacity of the region, and of the logic of nationalism itself, to deliver social and economic benefits to individuals and groups.

Although all technologies have modernizing effects, these effects vary by medium according to the relative administrative centralization with which they become associated and the habits of individual use that their material form encourages. As we saw in the work of B. Anderson (1996), the national orientation of print, and particularly the newspaper, created markets for a particular culture and language, which could then be exploited by a relatively centralized system of state administration. The newspaper provided a cultural idiom within which a high literate culture could develop. Although it did not do so in every instance, such a distinctive culture had the potential to become aligned with a state. The newspaper created a common cultural idiom that was simultaneous, albeit not fully simultaneous in the way that the radio was to introduce. Ideas that appeared in the pages of the newspaper were developed over months and years. The daily edition of the newspaper was read at different times during the day, or even left to the end of the week. An asynchronous method of achieving a common "national" experience was achieved through the material form of the newspaper. The newspaper's material form, though appearing fragile, turns out to be remarkably stable and enduring. We can still visit the archives to read newspapers preserved from the eighteenth and nineteenth centuries.

In an important transformation that intensified the effects of the newspaper, the telegraph allowed for the simultaneity of experience that would become the hallmark of later media punctuations. Economic markets were changed irrevocably. The practice of arbitrage was to become more difficult after the telegraph. Buying low in one geographic area in order to sell high in another certainly continued after the introduction of the telegraph, but thereafter most hedging against changes in price occurred over time, not in space (Carey 2003). National institutions to facilitate the price system followed, including the stock exchange, but also the chain department store and franchise operation, with prices offered consistently across a national space. In the same way that the telegraph had done, the telephone moved the habits of daily, simultaneous communication to the homes of individuals. National systems of infrastructure to facilitate communication with a growing and increasingly homogenous national market were created – some by private companies, but most by state organizations.

The advent of radio, as we have seen, began in regional settings but eventually was to signal a national orientation to the regulation and ultimate uses of communications technologies, as did television. Each medium in succession created a mass audience that participated more intensively in real time, and the more intensive simultaneity contributed to the creation of a more "national" audience. When broadcast in the 1940s, for example, the *Canadian Farm Radio Forum* could be understood but not fully appreciated in its social meaning outside of Canada, even by foreign English-speaking audiences. Likewise, those listening from north of the border to one of the US Office of Education's radio broadcasts during the 1930s could only have a general sense of the program's national meaning for the US audience.

Radio, like the newspaper, was initially associated with individual reception. The listener was required to remain silent and still while trying to discern the weak signal of the early radio receivers. As the radio's broadcasting signal gathered strength and as the quality of receivers increased, radio listening took on something of the nature of visiting the public library: at once solitary and communal. The audience made up of individuals quickly gave way to small groups of people listening around the family radio set, creating a public-private experience that is still today part of radio's ethos. The radio listener is independent but is also a co-actor within a public space. Radio involves the "writer-speaker," the narrator and commentator whose sensibility is rooted in the written word, which is spoken aloud for the benefit of the listening audience. This combination of the ancient oral tradition and the modern mode of an electric medium and the literate sensibility of the writer-speaker suggests something of radio's transitional role in national movements. Through radio the oral and the textual meet, combine, and compete. In this way, a popular foundation is prepared for the development of a high literate culture.

With each medium in history, then, the effects on social practices and the eventual implications for national culture varied. This was so in part because of the senses that were called upon by each medium. Print instilled the habits of solitary reflection and analysis through the focused attention required of the eye. The radio allowed for individuals to do other things while listening, but this heightened the experience of hearing things as they happened in real time. With radio and television, important events in the news were heard while individuals were going about their daily routine, invoking the popular question, *Where were you, or what were you doing, when...*

The effects of new communications technologies varied as well because of their cumulative effect. A new medium was experienced in the context of previous media, and the content of the new medium was the medium it was supplanting, a phenomenon that McLuhan called the "rearview mirror" (1964). A new medium's content is that of an older medium. The new medium of radio was primarily given to broadcasting the written word, and many of the first television broadcasts were of radio plays. There is a lag in the adoption of a new medium, and the rearview mirror phenomenon involves the extended process of transition from the use of one medium to another. Yet the transition is never complete. Radio did not disappear with the advent of the television, and even with the widespread use of electronic text we now have more print than ever. The medium that seemingly disappeared was the telegraph. Even here, the sliding banner of headlines on television news channels uncannily resembles the cryptic messages that the telegraph produced around the clock. The contemporary news ticker is of particular interest to those seeking to anticipate price changes – just as the telegraph was.

There has been a gathering of social energy with each new medium in history in the enactment of a nationalist logic of organizing in both national and regional spaces. The cumulative effects of these media have supported nationalism by providing a channel of communication for a national culture and by demonstrating the culture's emerging modern sensibility. The internet provides new opportunities for the development of nationalist projects. The nationalist logic of organizing entails the creation of a common linguistic idiom, which is used as the basis for pursuing the modern goals of literacy, education, communications media, innovation, and occupational mobility. The archiving capacity of the internet allows the assembly and organization of cultural information in new, more powerful ways. The interpretation of this information can be presented in ways that enhance or retrieve the symbols and artifacts of a national culture. In addition to its archiving capacity, the internet's capacity for the exchange of messages means that individuals and groups can coordinate their actions in pursuit of their political goals.

Individuals and groups develop local meanings about how and why the medium may be used. A medium characterized by high levels of ownership control, for example, is still subject to interpretations within the local contexts in which its messages are transmitted. A national community is made up of an aggregation of local and regional communities, and these communities have the capacity to interpret what they hear, see, and read in sometimes unpredictable ways: "Although a particular representation of national community may be communicated through a centralized media system, this representation will have different meanings depending on the social context in which it is received. Thus, any community that depends on communication (as all communities do) will be subject to interference and mediations that disrupt and contradict dominant, idealized versions of that community" (Hayes 2000, 20).

Small groups using the internet have unprecedented opportunities to cultivate the cultural knowledge needed for a nationalist project and also the means of political organizing to bring the project to fruition. However, the internet has become a distinctive media environment, and the characteristics of that environment mitigate to some extent the capacities of the internet for providing a welcoming context for nationalist projects.

The Internet as a Convergent Medium

Of the internet's radical innovations, its convergent characteristic is the most profound. The term *convergence* has two meanings in relation to the internet. For business organizations, various media are said to converge if they are owned and controlled by a large, vertically integrated firm. Economies of scale may be achieved not simply through ever larger and more homogenous audience preferences but also through the presentation of the same content in more than one channel. A bestselling musical recording may be used in a movie, on radio and television, and sold directly to consumers via the internet. Convergence in a sociological sense concerns the centralized control of texts that is facilitated by the use of digital, rather than analogic, master copies. The idea of an authentic version of a work was associated with the analogic paradigm. In the digital paradigm, sound, text, and moving images can be used separately or at once, but all are rooted in digital form (Beniger 1986). While analog media (LP records and tape recordings, for example) gave priority and privilege to the original cultural object, digital media allow for endless reproduction of cultural texts at almost no cost, and with little direct controls available to monitor this reproduction (Poster 1999). With the conversion of the spoken or oral word, still or moving image, to digital code, the original creation may be revised or refined, and it may also be reproduced repeatedly with few limits of cost or technical constraints. The power of the nation-state has been curtailed to the extent that digital culture has escaped the power to control it fully. If the state's defining feature is that of the prerogative to use force legitimated by law, some part of that force has been abridged.

The history of communications media in France features an overt resistance by the state to new technologies. The hesitation to adopt the electrical telegraph in the nineteenth century after heavy investment in infrastructure to support optical telegraphy in the eighteenth century has been documented by Winseck and Pike (2007) and Lubrano (1997). The Minitel terminals, a kind of early internet system, were kept in use long after their disadvantages in relation to other systems were demonstrated (James 1996). The Front National (FN), France's ultra-right party, was an early exploiter of the internet. It used the medium to publicize the party's views, which were that the mainstream media were conspiring with the government to suppress its views (Bratten 2005). Bratten identifies the FN's increasing competence in the use of multimedia from 1998 to 2002 as a key to the evolution of web use by the party: "The evolution of the discourse of the FN website from a compilation of demagogic rantings to a more clearly and rationally argued series of positions over the course of four years suggests that the party has become more sophisticated in its understanding of the internet. It has evolved from a tool to publicize simply the latest press releases and speeches, to a "narrowband" system from which to broadcast its positions using an array of media forms from print and graphics to audio and videoclips" (2005, 528). Bratten argues that partly as a consequence of the FN's strategic use of the web, the French Government eventually left behind its cultural and economic concerns and began to use the internet to counter the FN's web campaign.

In the same way that the French Government eventually acquiesced to the rhetorical opportunities of the internet, the capacity of the Canadian federal government to influence social identity through the CanCon regulations and other cultural policy will become weaker as content is developed and reproduced in disregard for such policy. Consider the blogs, webcasts, websites, videoconferencing sessions, and email messages of the internet that are not subject to policy regulation. The power of the state to influence cultural content through regulation of media can only diminish with the rise of the internet. On the other hand, the national government's direct subsidization of community-level content production can continue to create a space for national identity development, with an influence similar to that of the traditional museum. The Community Access Program in Canada, for example, has helped establish community internet stations and has encouraged the creation of websites that highlight local culture (Government of Canada 2006).

A key implication for nationalism of the internet as a convergent medium in the sociological sense – the creation of a single digital format for sound, text, moving images, and bidirectional communication – is that text and image together can be used to develop powerful messages about social identity. The computer becomes a television, a radio, and a newspaper. The storage and retrieval powers of the internet allow for the continuous production of cultural meaning. The convergent character of the internet has implications for studies of nationalism in part because previous media are incorporated into the internet through digitization.

Historical media that have had a formative influence on nationalism, such as the printing press, radio, and television, are all reproduced on the internet. Text, sound, and moving images are presented within the same channel. Since each converging medium is quite different in terms both of how it is interpreted by audiences as a medium and how its messages influence users, the proportionate use of various media on the internet may determine the rate and means by which nationalist projects develop. Video footage on the web of terrorist acts, presented by terrorists themselves, illustrates the decisive character of the internet in demonstrating a social identity. The prototypical means by which terrorist groups had previously announced their intentions was through the release of a published manifesto or communiqué. The preferred contemporary method is the streaming video, which delivers the effects of the manifesto, not its argument. The internet has the potential to allow for the endless repetition of demonstration effects of this kind. Unlike radio, in which the modern and the antimodern exist in tension, the internet makes room for both to thrive. The nationalist impulse is alive and well in websites and newsgroups. It is a modern nationalism in many instances, calling for the establishment of a progressive state. In other instances, it provides images, text, and the spoken word that revive the notion of the past glory of a nation, calling the faithful to remember and in some instances to take up arms.

The convergence of text with moving images and sound has yet to be understood fully in relationship to the development and promulgation of nationalist programs. A "textual pendulum" can be described in connection to the relationship of text and knowledge. The relationship shifts from medieval intra/intertextual study to modernist extra-textual methods, and then back to a postmodernist intra/intertextualism (Soffer 2005). Readers of internet material look within and between documents for meaning. Hypertextuality, the capacity to move easily within a text and to other texts, is a key feature of the on-line reading environment. The tension between modernism and anti-modernism that is at the core of nationalism's ideological program may be re-created through a combination of historical media. The storage and retrieval powers of the internet allow for the powerful production of cultural meaning. An edition of a seventeenth-century newspaper – or something from today's news headlines – can inform a new multimedia production extolling the glory of the national culture. Nationalism relies on the invention of tradition; the internet will permit new methods of realizing such inventions. Cybernations or virtual nations, such as Yugoslavia and Kurdistan, may thrive as nationalisms without benefit of land base, in the manner aspired to in a previous era by the pan-Chinese movement in Indonesia (Williams 1960).

Going Global, Local, and Glocal on the Internet

Digital technologies are changing the way that individuals participate in the development of social identity. Of particular interest is the relationship of local and regional identities on the one hand and national and global identities on the other. Robertson (1995) states that homogenization *and* heterogenization are characteristics of contemporary culture and that the challenge is to describe the ways that this is occurring. The nationalist project may use the internet for the recollection, consolidation, and promulgation of a national culture. The internet's capacity for access through time and space to an online "archive" of the national culture is unprecedented in the history of media innovations. The stories, songs, and heroes of the nation can be retrieved from historical neglect, presented for consumption, and, most importantly, revised continually as part of an emerging narrative of the national tragedy.

The modernist approach to nationalism depicts modernization itself as the broadest set of causal forces to which nationalists are drawn. The internet is an emblem of modernism, and its use is formative on individuals and groups. The networked computer provides a window on events and ideas that originate around the world and around the corner. Television provides a window to the world, but the simultaneity of television is always a mass phenomenon. The natural disaster we see on the twenty-four-hour television news broadcast is not much different in psychic effect than the photo in the newspaper. With both newspaper and television, a mass audience considers the events of the day. The time lag is notched up from the twelve hours or so of the newspaper to the hour or two of television. With the internet, the global and the local become entwined for the internet user. The individual feels at once the sense of being part of a mass audience, but views these events through the lens of the local and the regional.

For a news item in the newspaper or on television, the adjacent information and events competing for attention are similar in scale and scope, more news stories selected by editors. With the internet, what is competing for attention are the unending sales pitches, the unfinished homework assignments and email messages from lovers, the twenty-four-hour link to the workplace and the organizational surveillance implied in that, as well as the communities of affinity. In the din of the internet as a media environment, the message of the nationalist project and its call for cultural uniformity will certainly be less compelling in some ways than it was previously. Furthermore, existing nation-states have new powers, and these may be used to maintain their hold on dissident groups that aspire to their own state, as Beissinger points out: "The global communications revolution ... creates opportunities and resources for those who would contest states by easing barriers to the creation and functioning of networks and movements. Of course, these very same factors ... constitute powerful tools in the hands of states for nationalizing their societies, suppressing minorities, and defining boundaries" (1998, 181). Another way to state Beissinger's point is that the primary meaning of the internet in relation to nationalism is that social groups using the medium tend to become less, and not more, subject to the influence of other social groups. The relative impermeability of distributed networks – their resistance to messages from outside of the group – demonstrates that the internet is less a force for global understanding, as its more optimistic proponents claim, than for incremental resistance to openness. Local and regional groups that are small, robust, resilient, and relatively closed are likely to continue to form. At the same time, the dynamic of nationalism, viewed through the lens of modernization, is that of progressive accommodations of regional and local cultures into a national idiom of culture that can find an administrative home in the state. The internet is creating more global villages and fewer national communities of understanding. It is not fulfilling the promise of those advocates who saw the potential construction of broadly based social and cultural arenas in which intersubjective understanding would take hold.

The internet will undoubtedly be used by nationalists in the same way that previous media innovations have been used, but it will also allow for new points of conflict. Chan (2005) studied online forums involving migrants from the People's Republic of China (PRC) who were residing in Singapore. She found that the internet opened up a social space within which people could resist and challenge their homeland in ways they otherwise would not likely do. The internet also allowed forum participants to imagine the PRC as a superpower and an empire, thus enabling them to position their homeland in opposition to the perceived hegemony of the US: "The resistance that was expressed by the migrants online was fraught with ambivalence, internal contradictions, and fragmentations. There were moments in which the grassroots nationalism displayed by the migrants affirmed or co-opted the official discourse of the government on national identity ... at other junctures, the official discourses of nationalism and national identity were challenged, undercut, or reformulated" (Chan 361). The internet may in this way discourage the brokering and coordination of regional cultures that in the past have presaged the emergence of nascent nationalisms.

A National Culture on the Internet

The internet is itself becoming a kind of national culture, and this is a potential mitigating factor on the encouragement of nationalism. The use of language and symbols suggests something of the distinctive "internet culture" that has developed. Text remains the bedrock of the internet – in both the presentational (websites and other static postings) and the interactional (the message exchanges of various kinds). Although the internet has become a multimedia channel, the major portion of the material presented on websites is textual. The user of the web needs to be able to read. The internet gives children and young adults an implicit motivation to achieve a basic level of literacy. If you want to be able to use the instructions and prompts for online games, you have to read them. Visual and auditory symbols provide cues for the contextualization of text, and not the reverse. This is in spite of the steadily expanding availability of video on demand. The photos and videos that are on offer function as an elaborate visual display within which text is embedded. In the same way that the newspaper uses text to narrow the multiple meanings of a photo (Barthes 1977), the internet is a medium in which text establishes the primary meaning of photos, videos, and other visual display.

The language of use online is English, though other languages are used for the exchange of messages. For multilingual websites, English is usually the second language. Perhaps more importantly, the administration of the internet through the Internet Corporation for Assigned Names and Numbers (ICANN) is based in the US. The design of software, which is the internet's animus, is carried out mainly in the US. Furthermore, the world's education and training facilities for the teaching of programming languages and other aspects of the internet's underlying structures are carried out in English. Complementing English as the online lingua franca is the expanding set of paralingual hieroglyphs, the emoticons used in messages and postings as a shorthand for emotions. The use of the English language on the internet can be used, of course, to create a privileged position for English-speakers. However, a nuanced view suggests that English may be used as well to create an alternative to a shared sense of national identity. In a study of an internet site created by Thai women, Enteen (2005) notes that the use of English on the site "decenters the geography and language of the Thai nation in the discussions of all things Thai, enhancing the potential for the construction of a virtual community premised on Thai interests, rather than a sense of shared nationality or nationalistic concerns" (462). The use of English on the internet may also be used in such instances to broaden the audience and the pool of participants in the discussion.

The internet's predominant rhetorical mode is narrative. The internet has been the basis for much optimism for intersubjective understanding, based largely on the undemonstrated notion that persuasion is the common rhetorical mode on the internet. The much more prevalent mode is that of narration. To be sure, the admonition to click on the *Buy* button is everywhere, but the basis for doing so is rarely that of an appeal through persuasion. Instead, the internet's email, texting, and messaging carry endless stories of what has happened recently to individuals, groups, social movements, and organizations, along with predictions about what may happen next. Telling stories online is the pervasive method for partaking of the culture of the internet. These stories are at the centre of the corporate and personal blog. They are also the dominant mode in the multimedia websites that convey the qualities of organizations and the goods and services that they provide, presented through narratives, accounts, and anecdotes.

The sophistication represented by the production and use of the internet's hardware and software is unprecedented. In going online, a whole environment of modern technology is called up. This environment includes an available supplier (and an existing system of prices and transportation), reading proficiency for users, to say nothing of a reliable supply of electrical power. The networked computer as a medium represents modernism in ways that previous media now seem in retrospect to have only whispered in anticipation. The internet may weaken the potential of energies of new nationalist projects by providing a kind of alternative to the culture of a nation. The culture of the internet will compete for the loyalties of potential recruits to a nationalist project. In taking up the culture of the internet – the narrative texts within an English-speaking zeitgeist of capitalist democracy – a new nationalist project may create a hybrid culture but more likely will see its claim to cultural distinctiveness weakened. The internet has become an emblem of modernism, in the way that television did for half a century. The promise of industrialization that gave life to previous nationalist projects can never convey the urgency that informed previous generations of nationalists.

The Internet and Diaspora

The use of the internet for structuring some or all of a community's activities may be characterized as either of the two basic models described by Feenberg and Bakardjieva (2004). These are the "consumption" and "community" models. The consumption model involves searching for and retrieving information, which is made available for a price. In the consumption model, users rarely talk to one another: "Privacy, anonymity, reliability, speed, and visual appeal are desired properties of this virtual space, mobilizing armies of designers in search of competitive technical solutions" (1). By contrast, the community model represents "relatively stable, long-term online group associations

mediated by the Internet" (2). These associations are largely uneco-
nomic, providing returns that are connected to the community's values,
norms, and meanings (Etzioni and Etzioni 1999). An important example of the community model is the online diaspora community.

Karim (2003) writes that diasporic migrations of the last few centuries "were largely influenced by colonisation and trading connections
well as by the steady improvements in transport and communications"
(3). Broadcasting media have been used for the development of intra-
diasporic communications, but Karim points out that the internet
offers a means of bypassing the hierarchy of broadcast media: "The
extensive use by diasporic groups of online services like the Internet
Relay Chat, e-mail, Usenet, Listserve and the World Wide Web is allowing for relatively easy connections for members of communities residing in various continents. As opposed to the broadcast model of
communications, which, apart from offering little access to minority
groups, is linear, hierarchical and capital-intensive, online media allow
easier access and are non-linear, largely non-hierarchical and relatively
cheaper" (2003, 13).

Global diaspora communities are making use of the internet in
ways that are likely to change how national identity is developed and
expressed (Laguerre 2002). The creation of virtual communities by
diaspora communities is occurring at a rapid rate, and national communities will continue to experience the influence of this cultural
churn. Diasporic communities occupy liminal spaces, having left
behind one set of laws and customs and not yet fully finding themselves
ensconced within another such set (Safran 1991). They are "betwixt
and between." The internet itself as a virtual medium provides access
to liminal spaces (Shields 2003). These spaces are opened up through
the virtual's characteristics of the "ideally real," which may be contrasted with spaces that are "concrete" and those that are "abstract"
(29). Diasporic communities can experience plausible, realistic aspects
of the new culture while delaying or mitigating the "concrete" and
"abstract" aspects. They can thereby manage the risk of their transition
to a new society.

The internet is used variously by prospective immigrants and new
arrivals in many countries and has a function as well in assimilating
new citizens. Using the internet, the prospects for a new life are de-

scribed for migrants, the excitement of moving to a land in which opportunities seem to be available. The arrival is documented as a period of adjustments, disappointments, and changed expectations. The internet allows individuals to anticipate the prospects for their assimilation into a new society, make sense of the immersive experience of landing in and adapting to the new society, and then reflect these experiences back to prospective immigrants. The final stage is that of the immigrant looking back to the old country, providing a view of what prospective immigrants, as well as those who have recently arrived, can expect to find in their new home. The online diaspora may also convey the character of the migrant experience to the next wave of prospective immigrants (Karim 2003; Ogan 2001; Portes 1999; Portes et al. 1999). An immigrant's experience is provided as a life story, indicating the stages by which the immigration and acculturation are accomplished.

Qiu (2003) describes the means by which Chinese students living in Canada and elsewhere maintain contact through an online magazine. The experiences of diasporas before transplantation to the new country involve the events that helped to form the cultural interests they developed in their homeland. Tastes, values, and even worldview may thereby be connected with the experience "back home." Authors recall past experiences in China; they also refer to the affection they still hold for family and friends left behind. In this way, the magazine provides continuity with the students' cultural experience.

Online diaspora communities represent a means by which the internet may be used to maintain "horizontal" ties of affinity. Preferred ways of life must be recognized and acknowledged as rights of citizenship (Habermas 1996). Contemplating a "constitutional patriotism," Habermas states that such rights derive from the acknowledgement of the interdependence of individuals identifying themselves as conationals: "If ... the system of rights is elaborated and extended, each citizen can perceive, and come to appreciate, citizenship as the core of what holds people together, and of what makes them at the same time dependent on, and responsible for, each other. They perceive that private and public autonomy each presupposes the other in maintaining and improving necessary conditions for preferred ways of life ... They learn to conceive citizenship as the frame for that dialectic between legal and actual equality from which fair and convenient living conditions for all of them can emerge" (ibid., 291). The "private and public autonomy" that Habermas envisions might be developed in part through wide access and community uses of the internet. The internet is contributing to a citizenship based on an "articulation of the universal and particular at a level at once more general and more local than the nation-state," as Poster (1999, 239) describes it. B. Anderson (1996) took up the metaphor of maps to describe the practices of colonizing nation-states. In the age of the internet, we may return to the map to fashion an "alternative geography," revealing a "cartography of fractures which emphasizes the relations between differently valorized sites and spaces sutured together under masks of unity such as the nation-state" (Shields 1991, 278).

An expression of the use of the internet for the simultaneous involvement in identities at more than one level is the *community network*. Community networks bring people living in a local area, such as a town or city, into an electronic network for the purpose of increasing democratic participation in civic issues at the local, regional, national, and global levels (Gurstein 2000). They are conspicuous examples of the "community model" described by Feenberg and Bakardjieva, an alternative for the individual who establishes online relationships and joins affinity groups lacking local and regional meaning. Community networks have the potential to allow for the brokering of interests in the pursuit of social cohesion. Because the costs of community networks are not routinely borne by government, community networks depend on the efforts and contributions of their members. As a consequence, their sustainability is often in jeopardy (Ramirez et al. 2005).

The internet's influence and effects may be best understood in the context of previous historical communications media that preceded it. Our view of the internet's capacity for combining the effects of these previous media is still incomplete, but there are suggestions already that nationalism in the age of the internet will become less pervasive as a social force in some ways and more powerful in others. The tension between modernism and antimodernism that is at the heart of nationalism may become more easily negotiated by nationalist leaders and their followers using the internet. On the other hand, the political brokering and cultural accommodations characteristic of nationalist movements may become more difficult when online groups become more impermeable to ideas and influences from outside. The internet forms a culture of its own and may distract potential recruits to the nationalist project. The internet promises to have important influences on national communities, and online diaspora communities and community networks provide a kind of foreshadowing of how the narratives of individuals in transition within national cultures will become a key feature of social and cultural life in Canada.

Concluding Reflections on Citizen, Region, Nation-State, and a New Form of "Publicness"

The literary critic Celeste Langan refers to modern artistic efforts to "attach" language "not to the soil but to technology" (1995). In the alignment of nation and state, the nationalist project makes "language appear as if it is, technologically, suspended in the air" (Mrázek 2002, 30). Texts are today part of media-saturated regional and national spaces in ways that were unimaginable when, in 1971, Northrop Frye famously distinguished between the cultural environment of region and that of the nation. Frye's conceptual separation of regional *identity* from national *unity* highlights the constitutive character of literary and other artistic texts. That texts are now in continuous circulation within a media environment of what Gerald Friesen (2000) has called "screen capitalism" is a decisive change. Because of their continuous circulation by media, national symbols may become part of a regional culture in ways that are both intended and unintended; in turn, local cultural concerns may be taken up as part of a discourse about national unity. The interleafing of regional and national cultures and identities seems likely to accelerate in frequency and intensify in effect, but the outcome in terms of national unity – Gellner's nationalist principle of the congruence of the political and national unit – is less clear.

It was noted that the term *convergence* has two meanings in relation to the internet. In business organizations, various media are said to converge if they are operated under the control of an increasingly large firm. As noted above, a bestselling musical recording may therefore be sold in multiple products: in a movie, on radio and television, and

in electronic files distributed using the internet. Convergence in a sociological sense connotes the tendency to centralized control that digital,
rather than analogic, master copies confer on the producers of cultural
texts. A key implication for nationalism of the internet as a convergent
medium in this latter sense – the creation of a single digital format for
sound, text, moving images, and bidirectional communication – is
that text and image will be used to develop powerful messages about
social identity.

The culture of the internet constitutes a flattening of global space
onto the plane of the computer screen. Even while the potential grows
for technology to organize and manipulate symbols in the support of
social identity, social groups making use of online communication
can become more insular in their concerns. A resistance to messages
from outside of the group suggests that the internet may foster less
openness to the nationalist project as well as to other appeals to social
identity that are on offer. The internet itself represents what may be
considered a new "national" culture. The linguistic idiom and symbols
used in online communication and interaction on the internet suggests something of the culture that has developed, which is English-
speaking, narrative, and arranged around text. The social identity that
is available through technology may distract many from the doctrine
and program of nationalism. We saw as well the potential problem of
the state in controlling digital cultural content. Through the conversion of the spoken or oral word, still or moving image, to digitized
form, the original creation is less subject to the power of the nation-
state to legal sanctions for use within national boundaries. The historical defining feature of the state has been the use of force legitimated
by law, and some part of that force has been curtailed in the domain
of the internet.

The concept of *global cultural flows* allows us to examine the relationship between the powerful messages, symbols, and implications
of global media and the local creation of cultural and social meaning.
The direction of these flows is bidirectional, from the local to the
global, as well as from the global to the local. Even as it delivers the
symbols of global popular culture to people in local contexts, new expressions of language, dress, and music are continuously being taken
up from the local places in which they appear. Some of the concerns

raised by global flows are legal, in that with copyright law increasingly reaching out to determine who owns new places and words, creative expression may be dampened (Coombe 1998). Other concerns are political. For example, the status of individual continental cultures could be threatened by the European Union if standardization occurs through the dominance of mass media and in particular by the English language and the economic power of Germany (Morley and Robins 1995).

In his study of cultural flows and global political structures, Deibert (1997) theorizes the dual effects of a change in technologies. Effects may be observed in *distributional changes* and in *changes to social epistemology*. Following Innis, Deibert's distributional changes represent realignments in monopolies and oligopolies of knowledge. These are changes in social and political infrastructure, which occur as a consequence of the introduction of a new medium. Deibert argues that the distributional changes associated with the transition from the medieval age to the modern age coincided with the advent of print. They included an undercutting of the transnational power of the Catholic Church by the Protestant Reformation and scientific humanism. The printing press supported these changes by allowing for the effective circulation of new ideas to an ever-widening public. In the transition from the modern age to the postmodern, the distributional changes have involved reductions in the capacity of states. This has occurred as a result of the complex systems of production of transnational corporations and the creation of global financial markets. In addition, civil society networks are increasing their density and complexity, with members willing and able to bypass the state's conventional structure and to attempt, instead, to communicate with mass audiences directly.

Changes to social epistemology follow the tendency of a new technology to select some new ideas as against others. The web of beliefs through which people are socialized and see the world is disturbed by the new technology's introduction and use. Changes to social epistemology are inherent in Anderson's imagined communities. The transition from medievalism to modernism helped to create of a more autonomous individual. The new individual emerged as a consequence of new forms of copyright and authorship, the orientation to visual, rather than aural, media, and a group identity emerging in connection to a vernacular language. Paradoxically, the everyday language of *parole* continues to thrive while the systematic striving to create a more refined and formalized *langue* remains at the heart of nationalist activities (Fishman 1996). The postmodern age is characterized by an imagined community that is "hyperpluralistic and fragmented – the very antithesis of the modern mass community" (Deibert 1997, 195). Such a community may find more continuities in Canada than in other countries of the world (Castells 2001). Attention to such phenomena as the virtual communities of the diaspora suggests that pluralism will continue to contribute to regional and national identities in Canada.

■

Returning to the broadband projects that are planned and in progress in Canada, a social process must be created in which the question of redesign is addressed as a matter of priority. The events associated with the missile crisis considered in chapter 2 constituted a "strange loop." The Bomarcs were impotent without nuclear warheads, but arming them with warheads would undermine Canadian national autonomy – a condition under which they would be rendered virtually unusable as an instrument of Canadian defence policy. There was no provision for revisiting the broad outcomes of the technology or even to think about alternative uses. It is conceivable that broadband networks, too, could form well-trod pathways for the hegemonic exercise of power. Meaningful consultation on the design of the network is needed at the outset – with redesign, regarded in the broadest possible terms, to be considered as an essential feature of the system.

The access and new connections of a wired Canada are explicitly intended to lead to new forms of social integration. In encouraging wide access to the internet, the federal and provincial governments seek a cohesive national economy (Government of Canada 1999). The pragmatic strain of thought associated with such programs is clear. Canadians are to become fuller participants in a global economy through gaining fuller access to information and communications technologies. Yet the new connections of a technologically mediated world in which Canada will participate actively are likely to be characterized by old forms of alienation. Habermas suggests that it is possible that the "systemic processes" of a wired world will lead, not to a global village, but to "the fragmentation of a multiplicity of global villages unrelated to each other" (1996, 292). Such fragmentation may well occur not only between nation-states and free-trade zones but also within the confederal and regional framework of Canadian cultural development and politics.

We can consider a familiar institution as a means of conceiving a future in which technology has a key role in the constructive linking of local and regional culture with an imagined national and global community. The community library's history as a social innovation is remarkably long and stable. Community libraries in North America arose from a social context in which a public space for reading books was established as something that would feed and enhance the spaces in which oral culture was already the primary mode of communication. In many towns and villages in Western Canada, it was a women's temperance organization whose members insisted that there be a local space in which the library would support written traditions to inform existing oral practices and conventions. There was a perceived need to link books to oral education and conversation. One would feed the other in a complementary fashion. Books would be freely provided because there was an imbalance in the community. Community libraries were established as spaces for information-seeking. What was set aside at that historical moment was the idea of the library as a space for interaction, a place to consider new ideas and deliberate on potential community resolutions. Yet technology may allow for the reintroduction into the community library, or some metaphorical location parallel with it, a public space for interaction. Indeed, with the installation of public internet stations and the use of email in public libraries, people are increasingly using library spaces to interact, rather than only to find information. Although programming in the community library has always included interaction and dialogue – in the form of storytelling for children, public lectures, recitals, and book talks – the notion of the community library as a site for the exchange of messages is relatively new. Furthermore, although the typical user of the community library has been a middle-class, educated woman accompanied by young children, this "new" visitor to the library is often from the very bottom of the socioeconomic ladder.

The community library has in the past put up the written word against, or in completion of, the spoken word in community contexts. In spite of the process of media convergence which will result in more images appearing online, the internet is still primarily a text-based medium. Text will be with us for some time, because of its capacity to allow for focused thought and the development of the individual persona. Text is certainly not in short supply, thanks to text-rich internet browsers. The community library could become a central node in a network of public interaction and dialogue. Interactive media such as videoconferencing could become a complementary mode of interaction for online groups. The community library could become a primary site for such interaction. Online communities could claim and use the virtual and geographical space of the community library in order to converse, critique, and create.

A powerful aspect of the community library in relation to social identity is the simultaneously private and public nature of the experience. The visitor to the community library is conscious of the public character of activity in the library space. Materials and facilities are generally open to anyone. The design of the space incorporates a recognition of the public's free and relatively unmoderated use of the community library. Yet the act of reading is a private activity that, within the walls of the library, becomes moderated by "publicness." Visiting the library is an act that is both public and private, and this is possible because of the historically valid mandate of the library, the design principles of access and openness, and the appropriation and use of meaningful public spaces. It is possible to imagine the community library as a prototype of an open, media-rich national space that Canada could become.

The US novelist John Updike has visited and revisited a particular narrative subject and sensibility since his first novel, *The Poorhouse*

Fair, was published in 1959. In *Villages* (2004), Updike returns yet again to a description of characters living in a changing physical and psychic landscape over a period of decades after World War II. The characters are presented as a series of married and remarried couples who observe, experience, and contribute to the advance of sociotechnological change in the interstices of rural New England and its suburban precincts. Through the eyes of characters who are profoundly ambivalent to this change, Updike describes the steady erasure of rural landmarks and ways of life. Cities encroach upon and swallow up bucolic spaces subject only to the resistance of the passing in time of human generations – the rural residents themselves – and their habits and customs inscribed in such cultural texts as the mutating architectural forms of the streetscapes. Associated with these concrete obliterations is the remembering and forgetting in which characters engage.

At the centre of *Villages* is the most poignant and fundamental of changes for Updike's characters, which is the transformation of long-term, intimate relationships into a sequence of discrete interactions whose meaning and implications are reflected upon by the narrator. The stable family unit of the past, with its symbolic and physical violence, is remembered as having had the power to draw a previous generation into an extended web of family relationships – a tangle of meanings from which the characters have emerged, and which they continue to regard as holding an antique attraction. These remembrances are at once continuous with tradition and in contradiction of it. The narrator at one point realizes retrospectively that his own professional work, which has figured in a minor branch of the rise of computerization in the 1960s, was enmeshed with his motivation to engage in a succession of personal couplings and affairs. The intimate relationships have replaced the rural landmarks as cultural markings. "He wanted to have technology and illusions, too," reflects the narrator, "both were the ameliorative fruits of the human imagination" (199). For Updike, technology has implications for the construction of personal identity and for disturbances in all manner of human relationships and interrelationships. It is also at the centre of the continuous process of building a consensus regarding the legitimacy of social change.

It is through the meeting of technology with social change that we can observe that technology's effects. Such a meeting is a "kind of chance 'fitness' between social forces and ideas on the one hand, and communications environment on the other" (Deibert 1997, x). Technology has found a place in the Canadian imagination as an expression of a collective cultural project. It has helped "suture," to use Stuart Hall's word, regional differences by providing a view of social progress that is modern, endlessly adaptable to space and place, and amenable to the retrospective creation of tradition and social identity. The local and the regional have been conflated in the internet with the national and the global in ways that we cannot yet fully comprehend. In Thompson's view, this means everything has changed: "In a fundamental way, the use of communication media transforms the spatial and temporal organization of social life, creating new forms of action and interaction, and new modes of exercising power, which are no longer linked to the sharing of a common local" (1995, 4). Thompson views media-rich social spaces as offering the potential for a heightened sense of benevolence toward those whose fate we can learn about through the use of our computers, televisions, radios, and newspapers. He describes a "new kind of publicness" that media can foster. Its publicness is premised not on the interaction of co-present participants, as the ancient Greek agora was, but on what Thompson calls the "non-localized, non-dialogical, open-ended space of the visible in which mediated symbolic forms can be expressed and received by a plurality of non-present others" (1995, 245). Thompson argues that a renewal of public life is required. He develops the principle of *regulated pluralism*, which would recognize and protect the free expression of media institutions that are separate from the state, while ensuring that such institutions represent a diverse set of interests. Through deconcentration of resources in the media industries and through separation of media institutions from the state, the principle of regulated pluralism requires the direct influence of government.

Yet Friesen would dispute Thompson's claim that technology is completely redefining local culture and that everything has changed with the advent of the internet. He argues in his essay on the relationship of citizen to nation that the development of regional identity within a federal system of government in Canada is historically stable and likely to remain that way: "Yes, institutions such as the nation will change, as they have in the past, but for the moment the existence of communities in defined spaces, and the consequent indissoluble relation between community and place, an association consolidated by our political system cannot be gainsaid" (Friesen 2000, 218).

That social identity continues to be shaped by the physical landscape, natural environment, and efforts by individuals and groups to reflect on and try to understand technological change is an ontological assumption. But it is portrayed in the portraits of individuals that Friesen paints in his essay. It is depicted in Updike's novels. And it may be observed through the constructivist lens of Canadian history. Scholars of a previous generation felt it should be kept in clear view, by expressing the earnest hope that technology would be interpreted and used in ways that increased community cohesiveness at the national level: "Our immediate conclusion is that the old view of society, as an atomistic collection of self-seeking individuals concerned with their individual freedom and contracting together to form the institutions of the state, is an obsolete notion in the technological era ... This is ... a matter of collective common interest with regard to the use of the technology on the one hand, and the protection of society through its political institutions on the other. In this new environment, nationalists will feel particularly at home" (Rotstein 1973, 212–13).

If community and place are indissoluble, and the nation is not, as Friesen states, the future of technology in relation to nationalism in Canada must be aligned with the future of regional culture in Canada. A technoconstitutional nationalism would involve the creation of a shared national space in which individuals acknowledged their interdependence as Canadian citizens. The interdependence that is at issue here is not only economic and political, although the political economy is implied in it. Its legitimating function would follow from a conception of citizenship as something that is shared by all, regardless of life preferences. In practice, it might look like a return, not something entirely new. It might well resemble the outlines of the postwar welfare state, another period in which social legitimation became a priority for Canadian society.

Canadians might do well to return to a consideration of the chasms and cleavages of national life that have become known to us from other historical periods of disturbance. An idealist strain of thought on the dialectic of technology and nationalism would lead us to concern ourselves with – to touch on only the most intractable cases – continued attention to native claims for forms of sovereignty, a meaningful acknowledgement that some portion of the population will not or cannot participate in the marketplace of paid work, and a recognition of the intrinsic value of rural and folk ways of life. Recognition of difference and redistribution through the welfare state are not incompatible (Fraser 1998). Giving substantive attention to areas that are likely, in the postmodern social paradigm, to become more resistant to efforts to encourage social integration could allow the Grant-Cook dialectic to find continuing relevance. In this way, the historic, pragmatic accommodations of Canadian history, given priority by Ramsay Cook in his deliberation on the question of technology and nationalism, and the principle of national autonomy, given primacy by George Grant on the same question, might be accomplished at once.

BIBLIOGRAPHY

Aberhart, W. 2005. People and politics. Alberta Heritage Foundation. www. abheritage.ca/abpolitics. Accessed 11 August 2005.

Adria, M. 2003. Arms to communications: Idealist and pragmatist strains of Canadian thought on technology and nationalism. *Canadian Journal of Communication* 28, 167–84.

– 2000. Institutions of higher education and the nationalist state. *British Journal of Sociology of Education* 21(4), 573–88.

Althusser, L. 1984. *Essays on ideology.* London: Verso.

Amir, S. 2004. The regime and the airplane: High technology and nationalism in Indonesia. *Bulletin of Science, Technology & Society* 24(2), 107–14.

Anderson, B. 1996. *Imagined communities: Reflections on the origins and spread of nationalism.* Revised edition. London: Verso.

Anderson, P. 1996. Science, politics, enchantment. In J. Hall and I. Jarvie, eds, *The social philosophy of Ernest Gellner.* Amsterdam: Rodopi.

Appiah, K. 2006. *Cosmopolitanism: Ethics in a world of strangers.* New York: Norton.

– 1996. Against national culture. In L. García-Moreno and P. Pfeiffer, eds, *Text and nation: Cross-disciplinary essays on cultural and national identities,* 175–90. London: Camden House.

Armstrong, J. 1982. *Nations before nationalism.* Chapel Hill: University of North Carolina Press.

Babe, R. 2000. *Canadian communication thought: Ten foundational writers.* Toronto: University of Toronto Press.

Ball, D. 1980. *Politics and force levels: The strategic missile program of the Kennedy administration.* Berkeley: University of California Press.

Barthes, R. 1977. *Image, music, text.* New York: Noonday Press.

Beard, E. 1976. *Developing the ICBM: A study in bureaucratic politics.* New York: Columbia University Press.

Beissinger, M. 1998. Nationalisms that bark and nationalisms that bite: Ernest Gellner and the substantiation of nations. In J. Hall, ed., *The state of the nation: Ernest Gellner and the theory of nationalism,* 169–90. Cambridge: Cambridge University Press.

Bell, E. 1993. *Social classes and Social Credit in Alberta.* Montreal and Kingston: McGill-Queen's University Press.

Bendix, R. 1977. *Nation-building and citizenship.* Berkeley: University of California Press.

Beniger, J. 1986. *The control revolution.* Cambridge, MA: Harvard University Press.

Berland, J. 2000. Nationalism and the modernist legacy: Dialogues with Innis. In J. Berland and S. Hornstein, eds, *Capital culture: A reader on modernist legacies, state institutions, and the values of art,* 14–38. Montreal: McGill-Queen's University Press.

Best, G., ed. 1988. *The permanent revolution: The French Revolution and its legacy.* Chicago: University of Chicago Press.

Bhabha, H., ed. 1990. *Nation and narration.* London: Routledge.

Biggest and best of the West's largest publicly owned corporations. 1980. *Business Life in Western Canada* 8(3), 12.

Billig, M. 1995. *Banal nationalism.* London: Thousand Oaks, CA: Sage.

Bormann, E. 1980. *Communication theory.* New York: Holt, Rinehart & Winston.

Bourdieu, P. 1991. Identity and representation: Elements for a critical reflection on the idea of region. In J. Thompson, ed., *Language and symbolic power.* G. Raymond and M. Adamson, translators. Cambridge: Harvard University Press, 220–8.

– 1990. *The logic of practice.* R. Nice, translator. Stanford: Stanford University Press.

Brass, P. 1991. *Ethnicity and nationalism: Theory and comparison.* Newbury Park: Sage.

Bratten, L. 2005. Online zealotry: la France du peuple virtuel. *New Media & Society* 7(4), 517–32.

Broadbent, A. 2008. *Urban nation: Why we need to give power back to the cities to make Canada strong.* Toronto: HarperCollins.

Bruner, M. 2002. *Strategies of remembrance: The rhetorical dimensions of national identity construction.* Columbia, SC: University of South Carolina Press.

Caldarola, C., ed. 1979. *Society and politics in Alberta: Research papers.* Toronto: Methuen.

Calhoun, C. 1997. *Nationalism*. Minneapolis: University of Minnesota Press.

Carey, J. 2005. Historical pragmatism and the Internet. *New Media & Society* 7(4), 443–55.

— 2003. Time, space, and the telegraph. In D. Crowley and P. Heyer, eds, *Communication in history: Technology, culture, society*, 157–65. Toronto: Pearson.

— 1989. A cultural approach to communication. In *Communication as culture: Essays on media and society*, 13–36. New York: Routledge.

— 1963. *Communication systems and social systems: Two economic postulates applied to a theory of communication systems*. Urbana: University of Michigan.

Castells, M. 2001. *The power of identity*. Malden: Blackwell.

Cayley, D. 1995. *George Grant in conversation*. Toronto: Anansi.

Chan, B. 2005. Imagining the homeland: The Internet and diasporic discourse of nationalism. *Journal of Communication Inquiry* 29(4), 336–68.

Charland, M. 1986. Technological nationalism. *Canadian Journal of Political and Social Theory* 10(1–2), 196–220.

Chennells, D. 2001. *The politics of nationalism in Canada: Cultural conflicts since 1760*. Toronto: University of Toronto Press.

Ciborra, C., ed. 1996. *Groupware and teamwork: Invisible aid or technical hindrance?* New York: Wiley.

Connor, W. 1994. *Ethnonationalism: The quest for understanding*. Princeton: Princeton University Press.

Cook, R. 1995. *Canada, Quebec, and the uses of nationalism*. Second edition. Toronto: McClelland & Stewart.

— 1993. *1492 and all that: Making a garden out of a wilderness*. North York, ON: Robarts Centre for Canadian Studies.

— 1970, August. Loyalism, technology and Canada's fate. *Journal of Canadian Studies* 53, 50–60.

— 1966. *Canada and the French-Canadian question*. Toronto: Macmillan.

Coombe, R. 1998. *The cultural life of intellectual properties: Authorship, appropriation and the law*. Durham, NC: Duke University Press.

Corbett, E. 1957. *We have with us tonight*. Toronto: Ryerson.

Crowley, D., and P. Heyer. 1999. *Communication in history: Technology, culture, society*. Third edition. New York: Addison Wesley Longman.

Davis, A. 1996. Justice and freedom: George Grant's encounter with Martin Heidegger. In A. Davis, ed., *George Grant and the subversion of modernity: Art, philosophy, politics, religion, and education*, 139–68. Toronto: University of Toronto Press.

Deibert, R. 1997. *Parchment, printing, and hypermedia: Communication in world order transformation*. New York: Columbia University Press.

De Kerckhove, D. 1997. *Connected intelligence: the arrival of the web society.* Toronto: Somerville House.

Denison, T. 1901. The telephone newspaper. From *World's work* (April). Retrieved 14 December 2005: www.uiowa.edu/~obermann/endofbooks/telephone_newspaper.pdf

Deutsch, K. 1966. *Nationalism and social communication: An inquiry into the foundations of* nationality. Second edition. Cambridge: MIT Press.

Dobbin, M. 1991. *Preston Manning and the Reform Party.* Toronto: Lorimer.

Dorland, M. 1996. Cultural industries and the Canadian experience: Reflections on the emergence of a field. In M. Dorland, ed., *The cultural industries in Canada: Problems, policies, and prospects,* 347–65. Toronto: Lorimer.

Douglas, S. 2003. Early radio. In D. Crowley and P. Heyer, eds, *Communication in history: Technology, culture, society,* 213–20. Toronto: Pearson.

Dryzek, J. 1990. *Discursive democracy: Politics, policy, and political science.* Cambridge: Cambridge University Press.

Dutton, W. 1999. *Society on the line: Information politics in the digital age.* New York: Oxford University Press.

— ed. 1996. *Information and communication technologies: Visions and realities.* New York: Oxford University Press.

Eisenstein, E. 2003. The rise of the reading public. In D. Crowley and P. Heyer, eds, *Communication in history: Technology, culture, society,* 97–105. Toronto: Pearson.

Ellul, J. 1967. *The technological society.* Knopf: New York.

Emberley, P., ed. 1990. *By loving our own: George Grant and the legacy of Lament for a nation.* Ottawa: Carleton University Press.

Enteen, J. 2005. Siam remapped: Cyber-interventions by Thai women. *New Media & Society* 7(4), 457–82.

Etzioni, A., and O. Etzioni. 1999. Face-to-face and computer-mediated communities: A comparative analysis. *The Information Society* 15, 241–8.

Faris, R. 1975. *The passionate educators: Voluntary associations and the struggle for control of adult educational broadcasting in Canada 1919–52.* Toronto: Peter Martin Associates.

Feenberg, A., and M. Bakardjieva. 2004. Consumers or citizens? The online community debate. In A. Feenberg and D. Barney, eds, *Community in the digital age: Philosophy and practice,* 1–28. Lanham, MD: Rowman & Littlefield.

Fichte. J. 1931. *The vocation of man.* W. Smith, translator. Chicago: Open Court.

Fishman, J. 1996. Perfecting the perfect: Improving the beloved language. In L. García-Moreno and P. Pfeiffer, eds, *Text and nation: Cross-disciplinary essays on cultural and national identities,* 3–16. London: Camden House.

— 1980. Social theory and ethnography: Neglected perspectives on language and ethnicity in Eastern Europe. In P. Sugar, ed., *Language problems of developing nations.* New York: Wiley.

Ford, C. 2005. *Against the grain: An irreverent view of Alberta.* Toronto: McClelland & Stewart.

Foucault, M. 1995. *Discipline and punish: The birth of the prison,* translated from the French by Alan Sheridan. New York: Vintage Books.

Franklin, U. 1992. *The real world of technology.* Toronto: Anansi.

Fraser, N. 1998. Social justice in the age of identity politics: Redistribution, recognition, and participation. *The Tanner lectures on human values, volume 19.* Salt Lake City: University of Utah Press.

Friesen, G. 2000. *Citizens and nation: An essay on history, communication, and Canada.* Toronto: University of Toronto Press.

– 1999. *The West: Regional ambitions, national debates, global age.* Toronto: Penguin.

– 1994. Regionalism and national unity: The Canadian experience. In M. Singh and C. Mohan, eds, *Regionalism and national identity: Interdisciplinary perspectives,* 37–48. Delhi: Pragati.

Frye, N. 1971. *The bush garden: Essays on the Canadian imagination.* Toronto: Anansi.

Gabler, E. 1988. *The American telegrapher.* New Brunswick, NJ: Rutgers University Press.

Gagne, W. 1976. Technology and Canadian politics. In Wallace Gagne, ed., *Nationalism, technology and the future of Canada,* 9–51. Toronto: Macmillan.

Gasher, M. 1998. Invoking public support for public broadcasting: The Aird Commission revisited. *Canadian Journal of Communication* 23(2). Available at www.cjc-online.ca/viewarticle.php?id=455&layout=html

Gellner, E. 1997. *Nationalism.* London: Weidenfeld & Nicolson.

– 1994. Nationalism and high cultures. In J. Hutchinson and A. Smith, eds, *Nationalism,* 63–9. Oxford: Oxford University Press.

– 1983. *Nations and nationalism.* Oxford: Blackwell.

– 1965. *Thought and change.* London: Weidenfeld & Nicolson.

Gibbins, R. 1982. *Regionalism: Territorial politics in Canada and the United States.* Toronto: Butterworths.

Gillis, J. ed. 1994. *Commemorations: The politics of national identity.* Princeton: Princeton University Press.

Gouldner, A. 1976. *The dialectic of ideology and technology: The origins, grammar, and future of ideology.* London: Macmillan.

Government of Canada. 2006. Industry Canada. Available at cap.ic.gc.ca/pub/about_us/whatiscap.html.

– 2002. *The new national dream: Networking the nation for broadband access.*

Report of the National Broadband Task Force. Ottawa: Government of Canada.

– 1999. Industry Canada. Available at strategis.ic.gc.ca/.

Gramsci, A. 1971. *Selections from the prison notebook.* G. Hoare and L. Smith, translators. New York: International Publications.

Grant, G. 1986. *Technology and justice.* Toronto: Anansi.

– 1985. *English-speaking justice.* Toronto: Anansi.

– 1969. *Technology and empire: Perspectives on North America.* Toronto: House of Anansi.

– 1965. *Lament for a nation: The defeat of Canadian nationalism.* Toronto: McClelland & Stewart.

– 1960. *Philosophy in the mass age.* New York: Hill & Wang.

Gurstein, M., ed. 2000. *Community informatics: Enabling communities with information and communications technologies.* Hershey: Idea Group.

Habermas, J. 1996. The European nation-state – Its achievements and limits. In G. Balakrishnan, ed., *Mapping the nation.* London: Verso.

– 1989. *The structural transformation of the public sphere: An inquiry into a category of bourgeois society.* T. Burger, translator. Cambridge: MIT Press.

Hall, J., and I. Jarvie, eds. 1996. *The social philosophy of Ernest Gellner.* Amsterdam: Rodopi.

Hall, S. 1998. Who needs identity? In S. Hall and P. Du Gay, eds, *Questions of cultural identity,* 1–17. London: Sage.

– 1996. The question of cultural identity. In S. Hall, D. Held, and T. McGrew, eds, *Modernity and its futures,* 273–326. Cambridge: Polity Press.

– and P. Du Gay, eds. 1998. *Questions of cultural identity.* London: Sage.

Harrison, T. 1995. Making the trains run on time: Corporatism in Alberta. In T. Harrison and J. Kachur, eds, *Contested classrooms: Education, globalization and democracy in Alberta,* 118–31.

Hayes, J. 2000. *Radio nation: Communication, popular culture, and nationalism in Mexico, 1920–1950.* Tucson: University of Arizona Press.

Hayes, N. 1988. *Ethics management at Imperial Oil Ltd.* Case 9-86-C057. London, ON: Western Business School, University of Western Ontario.

Headrick, D. 2003. The optical telegraph. In D. Crowley and Heyer, eds, *Communication in history: Technology, culture, society,* 123–31. Boston: Pearson Education, Inc.

Hechter, M. 2001. *Containing nationalism.* Oxford: Oxford University Press.

Heidegger, M. 1962. *Being and time.* J. Macquarrie and E. Robinson, translators. New York: Harper & Row.

Herder, J. 1969. *J.G. Herder on social and political culture.* F. Barnard, translator. Cambridge: Cambridge University Press.

Hesketh, B. 1997. *Major Douglas and Alberta Social Credit.* Toronto: University of Toronto Press.

Heyer, P. 1988. *Communications and history: Theories of media, knowledge, and civilization.* New York: Greenwood.

Hiller, H. 1987a. The foundation and politics of separatism; Canada in comparative perspective. *Research in Political Sociology* 3, 39–60.

– 1987b. Western separatism in Australia and Canada: The regional ideology thesis. *Australian-Canadian Studies* 52, 39–54.

– 1977. Internal problem resolution and third party emergence. *Canadian Journal of Sociology* 21, 55–75

Hobsbawm, E. 1990. *Nations and nationalism since 1780: Programme, myth, reality.* New York: Cambridge University Press.

– and T. Ranger, eds. 1983. *The invention of tradition.* Cambridge: Cambridge University Press.

Hodgins, B. 1973. Nationalism, decentralism, and the left. In V. Nelles and A. Rotstein, eds, *Nationalism or local control: Responses to George Woodcock,* 39–46. Toronto: New Press.

Hutchinson, J. 2005. *Nations as zones of conflict.* Thousand Oaks: Sage.

Innis, H. 1995. Great Britain, the United States, and Canada. In D. Drache, ed., *Staples, markets, and cultural change: Selected essays,* 271–90. Montreal and Kingston: McGill-Queen's University Press.

– 1972. *A history of the Canadian Pacific railway.* Newton Abbot: David & Charles.

– 1951. *The bias of communication.* Toronto: University of Toronto Press.

Irving, J. 1959. *The Social Credit movement in Alberta.* Toronto: University of Toronto Press.

James, B. 1996. Beyond Minitel: France on the Internet. *International Herald Tribune,* 8 January 1996. Available at www.iht.com/articles/1996/01/08/minitel.t.php#.

Juneau, P. 1985. *Broadcasting: An essential element of sovereignty and democracy.* Ottawa: Canadian Conference of the Arts.

Kachur, J., and T. Harrison. 1999. Introduction. In T. Harrison and J. Kachur, eds, *Contested classrooms: Education, globalization and democracy in Alberta.* Edmonton: University of Alberta Press.

Karim, K. Mapping diasporic mediascapes. 2003. In K. Karim, ed., *The media of diaspora,* 1–17. London: Routledge.

Kedourie, E. 1962. *Nationalism.* Revised edition. New York: Praeger.

Kern, S. 1983. *The culture of time and space, 1880–1918.* Cambridge, Massachusetts: Harvard University Press.

Kieve, J. 1973. *The electric telegraph: A social and economic history.* Newton Abbot: David & Charles.

Köhler, H. 1986. The *flugschriften* and their importance in religious debate: A quantitative approach. In P. Zambelli, ed., *Astrologi hallucinati: Stars and the end of the world in Luther's time,* 153–75. New York: de Gruyter.

Kroker, A. 2004. *The will to technology and the culture of nihilism: Heidegger, Nietzsche, and Marx.* Toronto: University of Toronto Press.

– 1984. *Technology and the Canadian mind: Innis/McLuhan/Grant.* Montreal: New World Perspectives.

Kymlicka, W. 1995. *Multicultural citizenship: A liberal theory of minority rights.* Oxford: Clarendon.

Lacan, J. 1981. *The four fundamental concepts of psycho-analysis.* J. Miller, translator. London: Norton.

Laguerre, M. 2002. *Virtual diasporas: A new frontier of national security.* The Nautilus Project on Virtual Diasporas. Retrieved 5 December 2005, from www.nautilus.org/gps/virtual-diasporas/paper/Laguerre.html.

Laitin, D. 1998a. *Identity in formation: The Russian speaking populations in the near abroad.* Ithaca: Cornell University Press.

– 1998b. Nationalism and language: a post-Soviet perspective. In J. Hall, ed., *The state of the nation: Ernest Gellner and the theory of nationalism,* 135–57. Cambridge: Cambridge University Press.

Langan, C. 1995. *Vagrancy: Wordsworth and the simulation of freedom.* Cambridge: Cambridge University Press.

Latour, B. 1996. On interobjectivity. *Mind, culture, and activity* 34, 228–45.

Laycock, D. 1990. *Populism and democratic thought in the Canadian Prairies, 1910 to 1945.* Toronto: University of Toronto Press.

Lessnoff, M. 2002. *Ernest Gellner and modernity.* Cardiff: University of Wales Press.

Lubrano, A. 1997. *The telegraph: How technology innovation caused social change.* New York: Garland Publishing, Inc.

MacKay, D. 1992. *The people's railway: A history of Canadian National.* Vancouver: Douglas & McIntyre.

Mackenzie Valley Pipeline Inquiry. 1977. *Northern frontier, northern homeland: The report of the Mackenzie Valley Pipeline Inquiry.* Ottawa: Minister of Supply and Services.

Mackey, E. 1999. *The house of difference: Cultural politics and national identity in Canada.* London: Routledge.

Macpherson, C. 1953. *Democracy in Alberta: The theory and practice of a quasi-party system.* Toronto: University of Toronto Press.

Mann, M. 2005. *The dark side of democracy: Explaining ethnic cleansing.* Cambridge: Cambridge University Press.

– 1996. The emergence of modern European nationalism. In J. Hall and I. Jarvie, eds, *The social philosophy of Ernest Gellner.* Amsterdam: Rodopi.

Manning, E. 2003. *Ephemeral territories: Representing nation, home, and identity in Canada.* Minneapolis: University of Minnesota Press.

McLuhan, M. 1964. *Understanding media: The extensions of man.* New York: New American Library.

– and E. McLuhan. 1988. *The laws of media: The new science.* Toronto: University of Toronto Press.

Massey Commission. 1951. *Royal Commission on National Development in the Arts, Letters and Sciences.* Ottawa: The Commission.

Memorandum to Prime Minister King, 5 November 1943, quoted in R. Faris, The passionate educators: Voluntary associations and the struggle for control of adult educational broadcasting in Canada 1919–52, 105. Toronto: Peter Martin Associates.

Morley, D., and K. Robins. 1995. *Spaces of identity: Global media, electronic landscapes and cultural boundaries.* London: Routledge.

Morris, M. 1992. On the beach. In L. Grossberg, C. Nelson, and P. Treichler, eds, *Cultural studies*, 450–72. New York: Routledge.

Mosco, V. 1996. *The political economy of communication: Rethinking and renewal.* London: Sage.

– 1979. *Broadcasting in the United States: Innovative challenge and organizational control.* Norwood, NJ: Ablex.

Mouzelis, N. 1998. Definitional and methodological issues. In J. Hall, ed., *The state of the nation: Ernest Gellner and the theory of nationalism*, 158–65. Cambridge: Cambridge University Press.

Mrázek, R. 2002. *Engineers of happy land: Technology and nationalism in a colony.* Princeton: Princeton University Press.

Nelles, V., and A. Rotstein, eds. 1973. *Nationalism or local control: Responses to George Woodcock.* Toronto: New Press.

Newman, P. 1973. *Renegade in power: The Diefenbaker years.* Toronto: McClelland & Stewart.

Nietzsche, F. 2005. *The Anti-Christ, Ecce homo, Twilight of the idols, and other writings.* R. Ridley and J. Norman, eds. J. Norman, translator. Cambridge: Cambridge University Press.

– 2001. *The gay science: With a prelude in German rhymes and an appendix of songs.* B. Williams, ed. J. Nauckhoff and A. Caro, translators. Cambridge: Cambridge University Press.

Noble, D. 1999. *The religion of technology: The divinity of man and the spirit of invention.* New York: Penguin.

Ogan, C. 2001. *Communication and identity in the diaspora: Turkish migrants in Amsterdam and their use of media.* Lanham, MD: Lexington.

O'Leary, B. 1998. A critical overview. In J. Hall, ed., *The state of the nation: Ernest Gellner and the theory of nationalism*, 40–90. Cambridge: Cambridge University Press.

Ong, J. 2002. *Orality and literacy: The technologizing of the word*. London: Routledge.

– 1967. Nationalism and Darwin. From *In the human grain: Further explorations of contemporary culture*, 83–98. New York: Macmillan.

Osborne, B. 2006a. From native pines to diasporic geese: Placing culture, setting our sites, locating identity in a transnational Canada. *Canadian Journal of Communication* 31, 147–75.

– 2006b. The place of memory and identity. *Diversities* 1(1), 9–13.

– 2002. Locating identity: Landscapes of memory. *Choice* 39 (11/12), 1903–11.

Osborne, B. and R. Pike. 2004. Lowering "the walls of oblivion": The revolution in postal communications in Central Canada, 1851–1911. In D. Robinson, ed., *Communication history in Canada*, 44–52. Oxford: Oxford University Press.

Panitch, L. 1979. The development of corporatism in liberal democracies. In P. Schmitter and G. Lehmbruck, eds, *Trends towards corporatist political sociology*, 119–46. Beverly Hills: Sage.

Peers, F. 1969. *The politics of Canadian broadcasting, 1920–1951*. Toronto: University of Toronto Press.

Pickersgill, J. 2001. *Louis St Laurent*. Markham: Fitzhenry & Whiteside.

Portes, L. 1999. Conclusion: Towards a new world – the origins and effects of transnational activities. *Ethnic and Racial Studies* 22(2), 463–77.

Portes, A., L. Guarnizo, and P. Landolt. 1999. The study of transnationalism: Pitfalls and promise of an emergent research field. *Ethnic and Racial Studies* 22(2), 217–37.

Poster, M. 1999. National identities and communications technologies. *The Information Society* 15, 235–40.

Powe, B. 1993. *A tremendous Canada of light*. Toronto: Coach House Press.

Pratt, M. 1992. *Imperial eyes: Travel writing and transculturation*. London: Routledge.

Province of Alberta. Alberta SuperNet is now operational throughout the province. www.albertasupernet.ca/. Accessed 24 August 2006.

Pugliese, D. 2003. Weapons in space. *Ottawa Citizen*. Saturday, 18 October 2003.

Qiu, H. 2003. Communication among knowledge diasporas: Online magazines of expatriate Chinese students. In K. Karim, ed., *The media of diaspora*, 148–61. London: Routledge.

Raboy, M. 1990. *Missed opportunities: The story of Canada's broadcasting policy*. Kingston, ON: McGill-Queen's University Press.

Ramirez, R., H. Aitkin, G. Kora, and D. Richardson. 2005. Community engagement, performance measurement, and sustainability: Experiences from

Canadian community-based networks. *Canadian Journal of Communication* 30, 259–79.

Reichwein, P. 2005. Holiday at the Banff School of Fine Arts: The cinematic production culture, nature, and nation in the Canadian Rockies, 1945–1952. *Journal of Canadian Studies* 39, winter, 49–69.

Richards, J., and L. Pratt. 1979. *Prairie capitalism: Power and influence in the new west.* Toronto: McClelland & Stewart Limited.

Ringer, F. 1992. *Fields of knowledge: French academic culture in comparative perspective, 1890–1920.* Cambridge: Cambridge University Press.

Robertson, R. 1995. Glocalization: Time-space and homogeneity-heterogeneity. In M. Featherstone, S. Lash, and R. Robertson, eds, *Global modernities,* 25–44. London: Sage.

Rogers, E. 1995. *Diffusion of innovations.* New York: Free Press.

Romanyshyn, R. 2004. *Technology as symptom and dream.* Hove and New York: Brunner-Routledge.

Rotstein, A. 1973. *The precarious homestead: Essays on economics, technology and nationalism.* Toronto: New Press.

Safran, W. 1991. Diasporas in modern societies: Myths of homeland and return. *Diaspora* 1(1), 83–99.

Schmitter, P. 1993. Corporatism. In J. Krieger, ed., *The Oxford companion to politics of the world,* 195–8. Oxford: Oxford University Press.

Schultz, H. 1964. Portrait of a premier: William Aberhart. *Canadian Historical Review* 45(3), 185–211.

Sharpe, S., R. Gibbins, J. Marsh, and H. Edwards. 2005. *Alberta: A state of mind.* Toronto: Key Porter.

Shields, R. 2003. *The virtual.* New York: Routledge.

– 1991. *Places on the margin: Alternative geographies of modernity.* London: Routledge.

Smith, A. 2000. *The nation in history: Historiographical debates about ethnicity and nationalism.* Cambridge: Polity Press.

– 1998. *Nationalism and modernism: A critical survey of recent theories of nations and nationalism.* London: Routledge.

– 1987. *The ethnic origin of nations.* New York: Basil Blackwell.

– 1981. *The ethnic revival in the modern world.* Cambridge: Cambridge University Press.

Smothers, N.P. 1990. Patterns of Japanese strategy: strategic combinations of strategies. *Strategic Management Journal* 11, 521–33.

Smythe, D. 1981. *Dependency road: Communications, capitalism, consciousness, and Canada.* Norwood, NJ: Ablex.

Soffer, O. 2005. The textual pendulum. *Communication Theory* 15(3), 266–91.

Standage, T. 1999. *The Victorian Internet.* New York: Berkley Books.

Sterling, C., and J. Kittross. 2003. In D. Crowley and P. Heyer, eds, *Communication in history: Technology, culture, society*, 220–30. Toronto: Pearson.

Strum, S. & Latour, B. 1987. The meanings of social: From baboons to humans. *Information sur les sciences sociales* 26, 783–802.

Taft, K. 1999. *Light among the shadows: The re-regulation of the electrical industry and the future of EPCOR.* Edmonton: Parkland Institute.

Taminiaux, P. 1996. Sacred text, sacred nation. In L. García-Moreno and P. Pfeiffer, eds, *Text and nation: Cross-disciplinary essays on cultural and national identities*, 91–104. London: Camden House.

Taylor, C. 1998. Nationalism and modernity. In J. Hall, ed., *The state of the nation: Ernest Gellner and the theory of nationalism*, 191–218. Cambridge: Cambridge University Press.

— 1993. Why do nations have to become states? In C. Taylor, *Reconciling the solitudes: Essays on Canadian federalism and nationalism*, 40–58. Montreal: McGill-Queen's University Press.

Taylor, J., and E. Van Every. 2000. *The emergent organization: Communication as its site and surface.* Mahwah: Lawrence Erlbaum Associates.

Thompson, J. 1995. *The media and modernity: A social theory of the media.* Stanford: Stanford University Press.

— 1991. Editor's introduction. In P. Bourdieu, *Language and symbolic power*, J. Thompson, ed. R. Gino and M. Adamson, translators, 1–31. Cambridge: Harvard University Press.

Updike, J. 2004. *Villages.* New York: Knopf.

van den Berghe, P. 1981. *The ethnic phenomenon.* New York: Elsevier.

van den Bossche, G. 2003. Is there nationalism after Ernest Gellner? An exploration of methodological choices. *Nations and Nationalism* 9(4), 491–509.

Vickers, J. 1994. Liberating theory in Canadian studies. In T. Goldie, C. Lambert, and R. Lorimer, eds, *Canada – Theoretical discourse/Discours théoriques*, 351–71. Montreal: Association for Canadian Studies.

Vipond, M. 1992. *Listening in: The first decade of Canadian broadcasting.* Montreal: McGill-Queen's University Press.

Walmark, B. 2005. KiHS: Bridging the traditional and virtual classroom in Canada's First Nation schools. *Journal of Community Informatics* 1(3).

Watkins, M. 1966. Technology and nationalism. In P. Russell ed., *Nationalism in Canada*, 284–302. Toronto: McGraw-Hill.

Weber, M. 1958. *From Max Weber: Essays in sociology*, translated, edited, and with an introduction by H.H. Gerth and C. Wright Mills. New York: Oxford University Press.

— 1930. *The protestant ethic and the spirit of capitalism.* London: Allen & Unwin.

Wiley, S. 2004. Rethinking nationality in the context of globalization. *Communication theory* 14(1), 78–96.

Williams, L. 1960. *Overseas Chinese nationalism: The genesis of the pan-Chinese movement in Indonesia, 1900–1916*. Glencoe: Free Press.

Winseck, D. and R. Pike. 2007. *Communication and empire: Media, markets, and globalization, 1860–1930*. Durham: Duke University Press.

Zabaneh, G. 2005. A critical review of the history of telegraphy. Unpublished paper, University of Alberta, 24 February 2005.

INDEX

deliberative democracy, 114

demonstration effect, 13, 90, 95, 136–42, 157

Denison, T., 38

Deutsch, K., 35, 42

diaspora, 170–1

Diefenbaker, J., 8, 56, 66

diffusion of innovations, 90, 138; two-step flow, 139

dikes, 35

Douglas, Major C., 118, 142–3

Douglas, S., 111, 113

Dryzek, J., 114

Du Gay, P., 27

Dutch Indonesia, 40

Edmonton Journal, 120

education, 24, 87; French, 88; German, 88; mass, 10, 22

Eisenstein, E., 96

Ellul, J.: philosophy of technology, 57–8, 68; *techne*, 64; *technique*, 57

Emberley, P., 21

English Civil War, 15

Enteen, J., 169

ethnies, 30

Etzioni, A., 171

Extension, Department of, University of Toronto, 130

Extension, Faculty of, University of Alberta, 120

Faris, R., 110, 113, 123

Federal Theatre Program, 120

Feenberg, A., 170–1

Fichte, J., 18–19, 93

Fishman, J., 111, 177

Fitzgerald, F., 153

Ford, C., 149

Foucault, M., 99, 107

Fowler Commission, 52

France, 26, 163

Franklin, U., 64

Fraser, N., 183

French Revolution, 15, 19, 36

Friesen, G., 79, 101, 124, 155, 174, 181

Front National, 163–4

Frye, N., 77, 106, 174

Gagne, W., 50

Galt Mines, 147

Gasher, M., 125

Gellner, E.: definition of nationalism, 93, 174; demonstration effect, 90, 138–9; education, 24, 87; high literate culture, 25, 95, 98–101; industrialization, 22–3, 25–9; innovation, 23; media, 97–8; occupational mobility, 23, 100, 137; theory of nationalism, 6, 8, 10, 12, 18, 70–1, 92–4

German Romantic philosophers, 18–21, 30

Gibbins, R., 8, 83

Gillis, J., 46

global cultural flows, 175

glocalism, 5, 156, 166

Gouldner, A., 48, 66, 96, 99–102, 111

Gramsci, A., 25, 28

Grant, G.: history, 59–60; "loving our own," 21; philosophy of technology and nationalism, 47–8, 51, 53–4, 183; secretary of Canadian Association for Adult Education, 124; totalizing effects of technology, 68

Grant, G.M., 61

Green, H., 55

Grierson, J., 121

Gurstein, M., 173